Words of Praise for
Hank Wesselman and His Books

SPIRIT
MEDICINE

Also by Hank Wesselman, Ph.D.

The Journey to the Sacred Garden
A Guide to Traveling in the Spiritual Realms
(book-with-CD)

Spiritwalker
Messages from the Future

Medicinemaker
Mystic Encounters on the Shaman's Path

Visionseeker
Shared Wisdom from the Place of Refuge

≈

Please visit Hay House USA: www.hayhouse.com
Hay House Australia: www.hayhouse.com.au
Hay House UK: www.hayhouse.co.uk
Hay House South Africa: orders@psdprom.co.za

Spirit Medicine

Healing in the Sacred Realms

Hank Wesselman, Ph.D.,
and
Jill Kuykendall, RPT

HAY HOUSE, INC.
Carlsbad, California
London • Sydney • Johannesburg
Vancouver • Hong Kong

Published and distributed in the United States by: Hay House, Inc., P.O. Box 5100, Carlsbad, CA 92018-5100 • *Phone:* (760) 431-7695 or (800) 654-5126 • *Fax:* (760) 431-6948 or (800) 650-5115 • www.hayhouse.com • *Published and distributed in Australia by:* Hay House Australia Pty. Ltd., 18/36 Ralph St., Alexandria NSW 2015 • *Phone:* 612-9669-4299 • *Fax:* 612-9669-4144 • www.hayhouse.com.au • *Published and distributed in the United Kingdom by:* Hay House UK, Ltd. • Unit 62, Canalot Studios • 222 Kensal Rd., London W10 5BN • *Phone:* 44-20-8962-1230 • *Fax:* 44-20-8962-1239 • www.hayhouse.co.uk • *Published and distributed in the Republic of South Africa by:* Hay House SA (Pty), Ltd., P.O. Box 990, Witkoppen 2068 • *Phone/Fax:* 2711-7012233 • orders@psdprom.co.za • *Distributed in Canada by:* Raincoast • 9050 Shaughnessy St., Vancouver, B.C. V6P 6E5 • *Phone:* (604) 323-7100 • *Fax:* (604) 323-2600

Editorial supervision: Jill Kramer *Design:* Amy Rose Szalkiewicz

Library of Congress Cataloging-in-Publication Data

Wesselman, Henry Barnard.
  Spirit medicine : healing in the sacred realms / Hank Wesselman and Jill Kuykendall.
    p. cm.
  Includes bibliographical references.
  ISBN 1-4019-0291-X (hardcover)
  1. Spiritual healing. 2. Shamanism. 3. Spiritual healing—Hawaii. 4. Kahuna.
I. Kuykendall, Jill. II. Title.
  BL65.M4W47 2004
  203'.1—dc22
                              2004000746

ISBN 1-4019-0291-X

07 06 05 04   4 3 2 1
1st printing, June 2004

Printed in the United States of America

This book is dedicated
—with deep gratitude and great love—
to
Kahu Hale Kealohalani Makua . . .

Me ke aloha pumehana.

Contents

PART III: Healing in the Garden

≋ ≋ ≋

"Our practice is not to clear up the mystery.
It is to make the mystery clear."

— **Robert Aitken Rōshi**
(spoken at Wood Valley Temple, Hawai'i, October 1987)

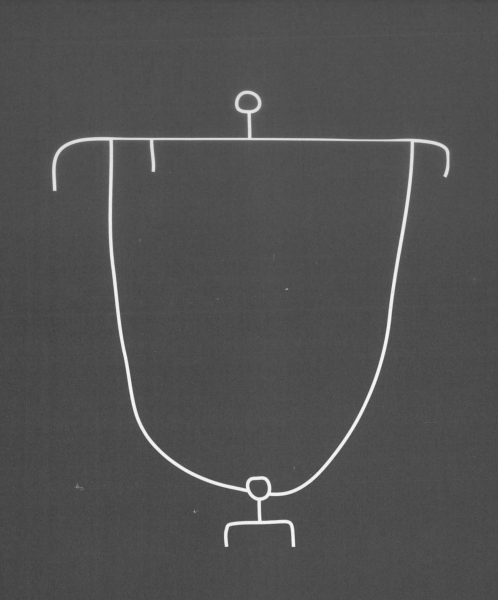

Introduction
by Hank Wesselman

$\text{A}\hspace{-0.1em}\text{T}$ the heart of spiritual awakening lies the discovery that each of us can achieve the direct, transformative connection with the sacred realms that defines the mystic. My previous book, *The Journey to the Sacred Garden*, guided us along a well-traveled path into this extraordinary experience, providing us with an effective, easily learned technique for expanding awareness and shifting consciousness safely.

The first goal: to find our sacred garden, a place of personal power in the spiritual realms, where we may enter into relationship with our spirit helpers, our guides, and our master teachers.

Here, in *Spirit Medicine,* my wife, Jill Kuykendall, adds her accomplished voice to my own as we enlarge our experience of the garden, creating a space where we may facilitate our own self-healing, as well as that of others. But in order to be a successful healer, we first have to know who we are.

Accordingly, the first part of this book examines the nature of the self from the view of the Hawaiian *kahunas,* providing us with an indigenous perception of how we're put together and how we function, deepening our understanding of ourselves and how healing actually occurs.

The second part provides us with a cross-cultural exploration of the principles of spirit medicine, derived from the perspective of an anthropologist who has spent much of his life living with indigenous peoples, and the seasoned insights of a transpersonal medical practitioner who has worked within the standard Western medical paradigm for 25 years.

The third part includes experiential exercises that we may use in our sacred garden, facilitated by the compact disc found in a sleeve inside the back cover. These *healing journeys* are drawn directly from our own experience and practice of spirit medicine and are designed to help restore balance and harmony, promoting well-being and good health within ourselves as well as others.

Throughout most of this book, our voices are merged, reflecting the unity of our shared wisdom, as well as our long relationship as husband and wife. Where the narrative is primarily Jill's, the text is preceded by **JK**; where the words are primarily mine, the initials **HW** attribute their source.

At the outset, allow us to say that we've been deeply impressed by the transformative power that spirit medicine conveys upon those who receive it, as well as those who practice it.

We've also noted that the real success stories involve those who take responsibility for their own well-being by embracing an active role in their own healing.

With that in mind, let's now proceed to make some good medicine together.

≈ ≈ ≈

PART I
Self-Nature

1
The Kahuna

JK: For several years, I was in treatment with a well-known Hawaiian *kahuna* healer named Papa Henry Auwae. Born in 1906, in a small community called Lapakahi on the Kohala coast of the Big Island of Hawai'i, Papa Henry was in his early 90s when Hank and I first met him. Trained by his great-great-grandmother since the age of seven, he'd been helping people heal for more than 75 years.[1]

Papa Henry credited the success of his work to *la'au lapa'au*, the plant medicines, but he also acknowledged that the preservation of life itself was due to *Ke Akua*—the transpersonal energy that permeates and animates all things, the same power that those in monotheistic religious traditions call *God*. Because Papa was intimately connected to this vital force, as well as with healing herbs, he had an exceptional track record for curing afflictions, and he claimed that he'd worked successfully with more than 12,000 cancer patients during his long practice.

A well-traveled anecdote recounts how an oncologist at a major medical center was diagnosed with terminal cancer and was given only a few months to live by his esteemed colleagues. At that time, Papa was visiting this center regularly as a consultant, so the afflicted doctor requested that Papa accept him into his care. With Papa's compassionate assistance and knowledge of herbal medicine, the physician's cancer was cured, much to everyone's amazement.

In the summer of 1999, Hank and I were able to facilitate a connection between Papa Henry and Larry Dossey, M.D., a major figure in complementary and alternative medicine, as well as executive editor of the prestigious medical journal *Alternative Therapies*. Dr. Dossey, in turn, invited Papa to present a keynote address about his work as a traditional healer at the fifth annual Alternative Therapies Symposium held in April 2000, on the island of Hawai'i.[2]

On the day of his presentation, the *kahuna* elder stood at the lectern and looked out at a hotel ballroom audience filled with physicians, nurses, and alternative health-care practitioners. Papa had brought along more than 150 of his students, trained in herbal medicine, who stood to one side of a long table covered with hundreds of medicinal plants. They offered a prayer and a song in Hawaiian, and only then did the revered healer launch into his talk.

Papa Henry proclaimed with great conviction that cancer is not a disease, but rather a cluster of symptoms created by a deficient immune system in combination with years of stress, dietary abuses, and accumulated toxins in the body. The room was silent as he described his treatment protocol.

At the physical level, this entailed a diet designed to do two things: (1) reduce the patient's intake of toxins and carcinogenic substances; and (2) lower the body's acidity, shifting its pH toward alkaline. This was necessary, he said, because cancer will not grow in an alkaline internal environment. Also included were a number of different herbs taken in carefully prepared doses to activate and enhance the body's immune system . . . and Papa had a working knowledge of more than 2,500 herbs.

At the culmination of his talk, the *kahuna* looked out at the roomful of hopeful faces and gently delivered the punch line. "Healing is 20 percent medical and 80 percent spiritual," he said. "This means that healing can only be done from a state of love. You can't do it from a place of fear. If you're not in love, don't do it!"

Papa's words reflect the indigenous perspective, and clearly affirm the pivotal role that positive intent as well as spirituality plays in healing. And there was also something else he said that day—something critical.

In treating a person who is ill, the relationship between the body, the mind, and the spirit is all-important, as this complex contains, reflects, and amplifies the sufferer's worldviews and lifeways. Accordingly, Papa's treatment protocols varied from patient to patient in response to each person's individual pattern.

Over the last ten years, Hank's books have drawn us into connection with many extraordinary people in the transformational community, including several elder wisdom-keepers among the Polynesian Hawaiians. So let's begin our consideration of spirit medicine by taking a look at the way in which this triune self is put together from the Hawaiian perspective, a view that has enhanced our own practice enormously.

≋ ≋ ≋

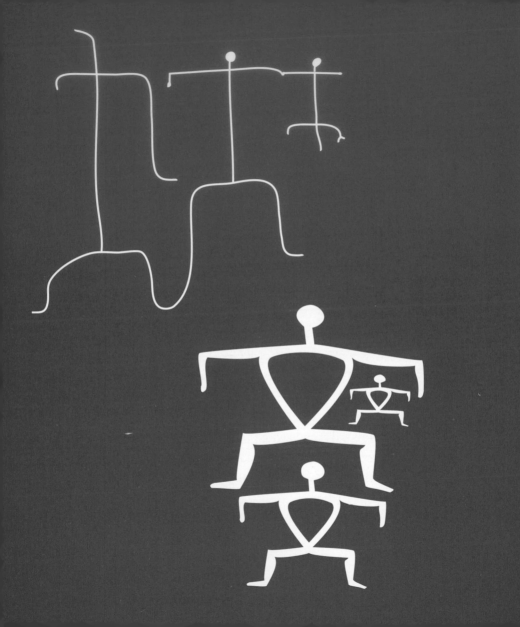

2

The Soul Cluster

HW: The quest to understand the self lies right at the heart of the Great Mystery. The Greek philosopher and mathematician Pythagoras was one of the first in the Western tradition to record his thoughts on the subject, and in the sixth century B.C., he made the observation that each human being is composed of three principle aspects: the physical (body), the mental (mind or psyche), and the spiritual (immortal aspect).

Pythagoras's insights on these *three principias* have influenced the words and thoughts of countless philosophers, spiritual seekers, and healers across the ages. It could be said that they find expression in our own time as Sigmund Freud's id, ego, and superego; and as Carl Jung's subconscious, conscious, and superconscious minds. The awareness of the triune nature of the self may actually have existed long before Pythagoras, however, because we find it among the traditional peoples as well.

The Lakota of the Plains Indian cultures of North America, for example, distinguish between a physical self, *woniya;* a cognitive self, *nagi;* and a divine spiritual self, *nagila.*[3] And the Inuit, who traditionally lived as hunters in the circumpolar regions of North America and Greenland, proclaim that we have three souls—a breath soul that we receive at birth (*anerneq*); a name soul that is given to us after birth (*ateq*); and an immortal, spiritual soul *(tarneq)* that is the true essence of who and what we are.[4]

How many of the indigenous cultures possessed this comprehension of the three souls/selves, and to what degree, is not known. After more than 200 years of assimilationist practices inflicted upon them by church and state alike, much has been lost. The examples just given, however, suggest that this awareness had its beginnings among the hunting and gathering peoples of antiquity, thousands or more likely tens of thousands of years ago.

And just why would our Stone Age ancestors be concerned with the nature of the self? Because in order to experience authentic initiation, you have to know who you are.

One of the early outsiders to investigate the spiritual wisdom of the Hawaiians was Max Freedom Long (1890–1971), a schoolteacher who lived in the islands from 1917 to 1931. His research, recorded in his books and papers on *Huna* psychology and religion, have found their way into many published works.[5]

Long chose the word *Huna* as the name for the Hawaiian spiritual traditions, referring as it does to something hidden or concealed. Many years ago, a Hawaiian elder, Kahu Nelita Anderson, gently corrected us and indicated that the word *Ho'omana* would be more appropriate, a verb that means "to empower" or "to place in authority," affirming the indigenous perception of the relationship between knowledge and power.

The Hawaiians acknowledged that each human possesses a lower soul/self aspect *(unihipili)* associated with the physical body; a middle soul/self aspect *(uhane)* identified with the mental or conscious egoic mind; and a higher soul/self aspect *(aumakua)*, our personal supernatural.

In life, these "three souls" form a composite, a unity within us that we think of as "the self," yet each is distinguished by its vibrational frequency, as well as by its functions. Correct relationship between these three souls is obviously essential. When there's harmony, everything works well. When there's discordance, there are problems to overcome and surpass. When there's ease within and between them, we're in good health; when there's dis-ease, we experience illness.

These insights reveal that the singularity that we think of as our *self* is really a cluster—*a personal soul cluster*. The word *soul* is used here with deliberation, rather than *self,* for each soul aspect is a part of the same totality, and each ultimately originates from the same source. And yet, as we shall see, they exist in very different states of quality.

Pythagoras would have found this perspective interesting when considered in relation to the Greek word *psyche*. In the historical perspective, the Greeks considered the psyche to be the organ of both thought *and* emotion. From the Hawaiian perspective, however, these two very different functions are products of two quite separate souls.

≋ ≋ ≋

3
The Spirit Soul

THE Hawaiian word for the higher, immortal, spiritual aspect of the self is *aumakua*, a term that might be translated as "utterly trustworthy ancestral spirit." It could also be interpreted as "the spirit that hovers over me," revealing why so many perceive it as a benevolent winged being or guardian angel. It is variously known in the West as the higher self, the god self, the angelic self, the transpersonal witness, the *overself*, or simply as the *oversoul*.

Occasionally, individuals who have a spontaneous mystical experience or lucid dream will find themselves in the presence of an immensely powerful and beneficent godlike being. The average person usually interprets this event, and attendant conversation, as a visit from a deity, a mythic spiritual hero, or even from God Himself, and we must always acknowledge the possibility that this may be so. But most often, the superhuman visitor and source of that *uncommon dialogue* is that person's own god-self, their oversoul.

Our oversoul is always in connection with us, throughout every moment of our life. The ease with which this connection may be activated reveals something that the indigenous peoples know well. When we're embodied here on Earth, the spirit world is not in some faraway, remote location. The invisible realms are all around us, all the time, and our oversoul can be accessed right here, right now, once we know how.

Our oversoul is in constant attendance, carefully watching everything we do, listening with concern to every word and thought, monitoring every choice and decision, silently applauding when we succeed, and quietly feeling concern when we fail. It never interferes with our life, however, nor does it ever tell us what to do. This is because the power of individual choice and free will is always honored. Exceptions do exist, such as miraculous avoidance experiences in which we're saved from an untimely end that's not in accord with our life's contract. Yet such events are rare.

Our oversoul may serve as one of our *spirit teachers*, and as such, it is the source of all the knowledge that we ever might need during our lifetime. It communicates best through the medium of *inspiration*, sending us ideas and hunches, dreams and visions, and revealing it to be the origin, as well, of our *intuition*.

Often when we sit in silence, a feeling of tranquility may begin to pervade us, filling us with a sense of utter peace. We may notice that if we consider some problem at such moments, the answer to the dilemma usually appears in our mind immediately. Our oversoul is the source of that feeling of tranquility, and it's also the origin of the information that arrives in our conscious awareness in response to need.

From the *kahuna* perspective, the oversoul is also the ultimate source of who and what we are, serving as our personal *creator*. In this capacity, it's the immortal soul-aspect that divides itself, sending in an energetic hologram of its essence that takes up residence within our body at the beginning of each new life cycle. This essence contains and reflects the totality of the character that we've developed across countless lives.

The divine breath (of life), what the Hawaiians call the *hā*, is the vehicle through which this spiritual transfer occurs. When we're born, we receive our *hā* with our first breath, and it remains with us throughout life until we release it with our last.

It is the divine breath that conveys our immortal soul's seed into our new body at life's inception and then carries it back to its oversoul source at life's end—an insight that's clearly reflected in the Judeo-Christian traditions that proclaim with authority that *God breathes life into form*. In Latin, the word for *breath* is the same as the word for *spirit—spiritus*. In Hebrew, the word for *spirit* and *breath* is also the same—*ruach*.

For the *kahuna,* however, it's not some monotheistic, fatherly creator-god that breathes life into us. It is our personal god-self—our oversoul, our own immortal spirit.

≋ ≋ ≋

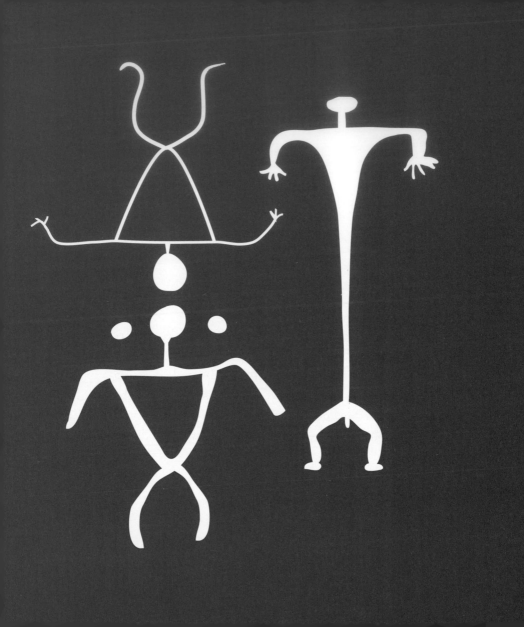

4

The Body Soul

WHEN the incoming oversoul essence takes up residence within a new body at the beginning of life, it encounters a distinct and separate "body soul"—a composite holographic field derived from both the mother and the father. This body soul is carried by the energetic matrix, around and within which the physical body has taken form in the womb of the mother.

On the biological level, when the two gametes, the egg and the sperm, come together and fertilization occurs, this results in a new genetic pattern to which both mother and father contribute. The same holds true at the spiritual-energetic level. The energy of the mother and that of the father merge, producing a unique spiritual-energetic matrix that carries ancestral imprints derived from both family lineages.

The first task of the incoming oversoul essence is to achieve a successful meld with the matrix of the body soul. Balance is achieved when this is accomplished, and the new personality of the individual then begins to grow and mature, manifesting quirks reminiscent of both motherly and fatherly ancestors. There are, as well, idiosyncrasies derived from our own personal ancestors—our past selves in former lifetimes. These are essentially soul memories that are recorded within the matrix of our oversoul. The merging of these three ancestral lineages—personal, maternal, and paternal—creates a unique form to our personality for each lifetime.

The body soul is thus revealed to be comparable to the unconscious or subconscious mind in Western psychology. From the *kahuna* perspective, this self-aspect performs much like a faithful servant in that it does what it's told. In the West, an appropriate analogue might be the inner hard drive of a computer, and this becomes quite obvious as we review how it functions.

For example, the entire operation of the physical body is under the direct control of the body soul. Our hearts continue to beat and we continue to breathe without our having to think about this because our body soul is responsible for these functions. These physiological processes include, by association, our biological drives (evolutionary software) and our innate, instinctual impulses (ancestral imprints).

As our personal inner hard drive, one of the body soul's primary functions is memory. In this capacity, it serves as the repository from which all personal records of our life experiences can be accessed. These include, by association, all our habitual and learned behavior (programming).

The body soul is also the source of our emotions and feelings, revealing why it's often referenced as the *emotional body*. It's through emotional response to our life experiences and the generation of feelings (reactions) that the body soul communicates with our composite soul cluster/self, telling us what it likes, as well as what it dislikes. In this sense, the body soul will *never* lie to us. It will always tell us how it feels—about this family member or that friend, about this job or that life opportunity. The body soul actively observes the outer world in which we live, as well as the inner worlds in which we think, feel, and dream. As the *body's mind,* it uses its five senses to gather information, revealing it to be our *perceiver,* as well as the interface between our self and reality-at-large.

As that interface, the body soul functions as the sender and receiver of all psychic experience, and is also the self-aspect through which connection with the spirit worlds is achieved. That inner portal through which our spiritual helpers and teachers can be accessed is located within it, much like a modem built into a computer. It is through the body soul that we achieve connection with all that exists beyond the self, including, of course, our oversoul.

The body soul can reason, reaching literal, deductive conclusions that are based on direct experience. These may be logical or illogical . . . but you only put your finger in a candle flame once. The body soul remembers what works, as well as what hurts, and in this sense, it's programmed to respond in a way that enhances survival. It is in this manner that we can grow, acquire new skills, and become more than we were.

With relation to spirit medicine, the body soul is the self-aspect that's programmed to repair the physical body when we suffer a wound or become ill, revealing it to be our inner healer. It restores us by reading the genetic code recorded on the molecular template of our DNA, and by following the "energetic blueprint" carried by the matrix within and around which the physical body is formed.

These two patterns, biological and energetic, are in relationship. They come to reflect each other, and together, they create the overall personal pattern that's essential to the maintenance and restoration of the physical body.

This pattern is necessary because the body soul is not creative, and it needs this blueprint to follow in making repairs.

Finally, like a good computer (or faithful servant), the body soul obeys orders. It does what it's told to do, and it functions best when it's given clear directives by the middle self or mental soul, the aspect that Western people often call the *ego*.

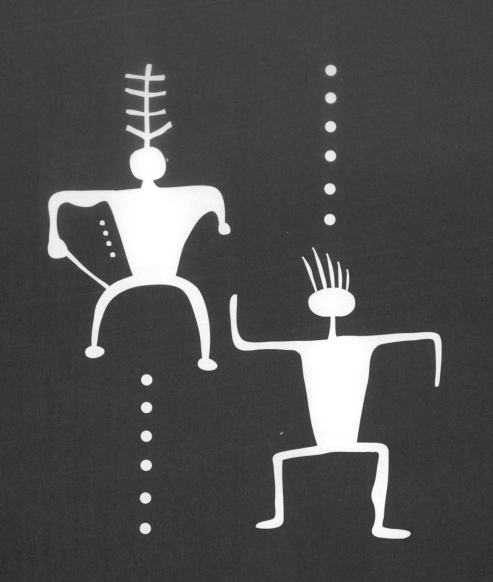

5
The Mental Soul

BETWEEN the oversoul seed-essence and the bodily soul, a third self-aspect takes form in response to our
life as we live it. This is the middle self or mental soul, the
intellectual aspect of us that thinks, analyzes, integrates
information, and makes decisions.

This is the *ego* as described by Freud, and the *conscious mind* of Jung. It functions as our overall chief executive, and as such, it's the source of our will forces and
our intentionality. This is our *rational* mind, which possesses full reasoning powers. It's also the source of our

creative imagination, through which it can produce new ideas, intentions, and thoughtforms of things or goals that it wishes to experience or achieve.

Considered together, these functions reveal the mental soul to be our creative, intellectual, rational decision maker and inner director—a self-aspect that evolves and changes as we grow in knowledge and experience. How well it directs depends on the beliefs it has accepted as so. If the mental soul believes itself to be powerless, one's life may be experienced in the role of victim. However, if it believes itself to be powerful, we will have quite a different life.

When beliefs about reality at large are accepted as unalterable facts, then the mental soul cannot categorize them as belief systems and may be quite ineffectual when confronted by the belief's effects. For example, when people believe they have an incurable illness, they may actually succumb to their belief rather than to the disease itself.

The *kahunas* consider the feelings and emotions generated by the body soul to be energetic responses to the stimulation of belief patterns, and as such, they inform the mental soul of the beliefs that are in operation, as well as how the body soul feels about this or that. The mental soul then has a choice. It can decide whether to respond to the emotions, whether to follow them through, or whether to reject them as invalid.

In this sense, it's obvious that a good working relationship between the middle mental soul and the lower body soul is essential. The mental soul is the master; the body soul is the servant. As our inner chief, the mental soul is motivated by order and tries to steer us successfully through the hazards of everyday life. It accomplishes its goals through directing the activities of the body soul that serves as its enabler.

In summary, what we think of as the self is actually a composite, a personal soul cluster of three functionally distinct soul aspects that takes form in each life. On the physical plane of existence, we perceive through our body's senses, conditioned by our anticipation of the future as well as our memories of the past. Through the vehicle of bodily consciousness, we experience the everyday world, to which we respond with emotions and feelings. The body soul collectively expresses our personality and perceives subject and object as separate. It's motivated by pleasure, moving toward things, people, and experiences that it likes, and moving away from those that it doesn't. Like a good servant or personal computer, it follows the orders given to it by the mental soul.

The mental soul (or conscious mind) includes higher aspiration and the intellect. It is the source of our will forces and works through intelligence to create forms of expression on the physical and mental planes of existence. The conscious mind thinks in extended space and time, gaining knowledge, true individuality, and illuminated understanding through its powers of discernment and discrimination. It recognizes the union of subject and object, rather than seeing them as separate, and it functions as the inner director and decision maker. As such, it's motivated by understanding and order.

Our oversoul is the spiritual source from which we emerge at birth and to which we return at death. This is the "god-self" who listens to our prayers and responds to our needs. It is the wise being who serves us as spirit teacher and advisor during life, and who communicates with us best through dreams, visions, ideas, and the medium of intuition.

This is our immortal self-aspect that provides us with access to the collective knowledge and experience of all our past lives, pooled into one holographic field. It is who and what we really are (there), continually growing, increasing and becoming more in response to the choices we make in our lives on the physical plane (here).

This process of never-ending change began a very long time ago, and it will continue as we pass through life after life after life during our long journey across eternity.

≋ ≋ ≋

6

The Human Spirit

THE *kahuna* wisdomkeepers know that we, as individuals, are part of a greater spiritual composite that they call *Ka Po'e Aumakua*. This is the collective spiritual essence or field of all humanity, formed by all the human oversouls pooled together. We often refer to it as the *human spirit*.

This greater human spiritual field could be thought of as an entity or being that carries within itself the wisdom of our entire species, *Homo sapiens*. Jung thought of it as the collective unconscious, and since we are all aspects or fragments of this field, each of us theoretically has access to this hoard of human knowledge and experience whenever we're in need of it. Connection with it is obviously achieved through our oversoul.

From the perspective of quantum physics, each human being could be thought of as a particle, with our oversoul as our personal wave-field that exists within the still greater collective wave-field of the human spirit.

From this view, several conclusions can be drawn with absolute certainty, First, each of us is truly a microcosm within a macrocosm; second, we're all interconnected to each other, forever; and third, when we're embodied, each of us exists as a point of focus within which heaven and earth achieve unity to become one.

Finally, through our personal oversoul field, in connection with the greater composite field of the human spirit, each of us can also make contact with an unlimited sea of energy. This is the power, the vital force, that shamans, mystics, and medicinemakers across time have always been able to access through the spirits or from God. This is the origin of the energy that Papa Henry called *Ke Akua.*

This power, available to us at all times, is far more than we ever might have need of to heal any illness, from aggravating chronic afflictions to serious life-threatening conditions. This brings us to briefly consider the physical body as well as its energetic complement, the energy body.

≋ ≋ ≋

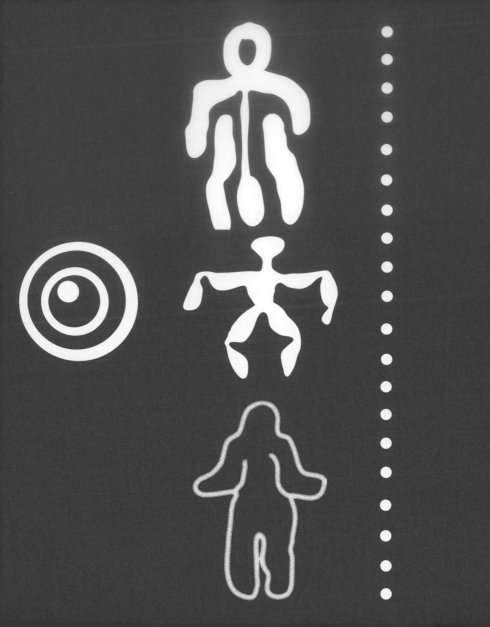

7

The Physical Body and the Energy Body

THE *kahunas* perceived the physical body to be a material expression of the oversoul in the same way that a painting or sculpture is the expression of an artist. This understanding is reflected in the Hawaiian word for the physical body, *kino,* a term that could be translated as "highly energized thoughtform."

This thoughtform is carried by an energetic field that has three sources: the energy of the mother, the energy of the father, and the energy (essence) from the personal oversoul. The composite *energy body* is derived from this triple union, and it carries the matrix around and within which the physical body is formed and maintained.

The Polynesians proclaim that the energy body (which some call the *light body*) holds the design for every cell, tissue, and organ of the physical body, and that it's this pattern that the body soul follows in making repairs. When the blueprint is in harmony, there are no problems. But if there's disharmony that distorts the plan, the body soul can no longer restore the physical, so illness results. This is why spiritual healers and energy workers alike regard illness as a breakdown within the body's energy system. We shall consider the causes of this shortly.

The energy body is also the repository within which all our personal memories, as well as our learned and habitual behavioral repertoires, are recorded, revealing it to be the source that the body soul taps in to for this information.

The growing awareness of this energetic self-aspect is one of the signatures of our *consciousness age*. Those with the gift of clairvoyance often perceive the energy body as an aura, as a bright and glittering orb that surrounds and interpenetrates the physical, changing shape and color with every thought and emotion. Western scientists, tempered by their habitual caution, still know little about it, although this is beginning to change.

By comparison, the indigenous peoples know a great deal about the energy body. The Lakota call it *sicun*, and they say that it's really a fourth self-aspect in that it carries the pattern of our life, as well as the net effect of the balance or imbalance between the dimensions of our soul cluster. The Hawaiians call it the *kino aka*, or the *aka* body, about which we will say more in the next chapter.

8
Levels of Reality

OUR understanding of the three souls, as well as the two bodies, leads us to briefly consider the multilayered nature of reality. At the outset, it should be observed that the number of these dimensional levels varies from tradition to tradition, according to how they're defined. Because our primary focus is on spirit medicine, only three need be discussed here, and once again, we will draw from *kahuna* thought for clarity. The Hawaiian Wisdomkeepers understood that the fabric of reality is composed of a multileveled vibrational field that is alive, conscious, and intelligent.[6]

Level One: This is the objective physical level of the everyday world that we all take so much for granted. It's a level of action in which our oversoul essence can inhabit a physical body—a level where we can have jobs and careers, as well as friends and families; build houses and accomplish goals; eat and sleep and make love; and so on. It's a level of challenge, and it's in response to life's contests that we grow and become more than we were.

We experience the physical plane the way we do through three basic assumptions that we accept as valid. The first is that everything is separate from everything else. For example, we're creating this book here, and you're reading it there, wherever you happen to be. This sense of separation between people, places, and events dominates our perceptions of the physical world.

The second assumption is that everything on the physical plane has a beginning and an ending. Your life began when you were born, and it will end when you make transition; stories and books begin at the beginning, and they end at the ending. This also reveals that on Level One, time is linear: It progresses from the past, through the present, and into the future.

The third assumption is that in the everyday world, every effect has a cause. Understanding the relationship between cause and effect is critical to healing and will be reconsidered shortly.

Healing modalities performed on Level One include all Western allopathic physical medicine, chiropractic medicine, physical therapy, massage, exercise, yoga, and acupuncture and acupressure. Herbal therapies could also be included here.

Level Two: The second level of reality (as well as awareness and experience) is the subjective point of mental-emotional consciousness in which feelings can be felt, thoughts can be thought, and thoughtforms created—the first step to manifesting something into the everyday world of Level One. This is also the level of energy, revealing it to be the dimension in which the matrix of our energy body exists. The mental soul and body soul are carried by this personal energetic field.

The first assumption by which Level Two operates is that everything is connected to everything else. The *kahunas* perceived these interconnections to exist as a vast energetic net or grid that stretches out across the continuum of the universes. This is the diaphanous weblike structure that mystics see in visions, and it's most likely the gridlike abstractions seen in indigenous rock art all over the world. The Celtic and Anglo-Saxon shamans called it the web of *Wyrd*. The Hawaiians call this matrix the *aka* field.

The word *aka* can mean many things in Hawaiian according to how it is used, including *shadow* or *reflection*. In this context, *aka* refers to the primordial stuff out of which everything, everywhere is made. In science, *aka* is analogous to what is known as *dark matter,* an invisible, undetectable substance that makes up more than 90 percent of the universe and exerts a mysterious force that holds the structure of physical reality together. Physics suggests that this dark matter is the scaffolding upon which the building blocks of ordinary matter assemble. These units of physical form are made up of protons and neutrons, and are generally referred to as *baryons*.

During the first several billion years of cosmic history, the baryons existed as vast gas clouds, composed primarily of hydrogen, which eventually condensed into a spidery network of filaments connecting galaxies and galaxy clusters. Stripped of its electrons, the hydrogen in the filaments cannot radiate light, hence the term *dark matter*.

These spidery filaments are the same cords that make up the web of the *aka* field and are analogous to the *superstrings* of advanced theoretical physics. It's likely that the indigenous peoples have known about them for a very long time because they're depicted in petroglyphs and pictographs that extend back well into the Stone Age.[7]

In *kahuna* thought, when you make contact with a place, an object, or a person, that connection is made of *aka,* a stretchy, sticky, invisible fiber that extends between your *aka* (energy) body and the *aka* of the person or place. It is through these *aka* filaments on Level Two that we suddenly know when the phone's going to ring, as well as who's calling; it's through these same cords that a close friend or significant other may tap in to our thoughts and may start talking about something that we're thinking of at just that moment.

It's the *aka* field through which psychic experiences occur, including extrasensory perception, clairvoyance, telepathy, clairaudience, clairsentience, déjà vu, and precognition. These are natural functions that we all possess to a greater or lesser extent, although some of us are better at it than others.

It's also through the *aka* field that shamans may communicate with plants and animals, with the winds and the rain, and with the river as well as the fish swimming in it. And it's through the *aka* matrix that shamans are able to connect with the spirits (in Level Three), as well as with the *mind behind nature*. The *aka* field is thus revealed to be the Internet of the second level. It's the real World Wide Web, and the rich legacy of rock art reveals that shamans have been utilizing it for a very long time.

The second assumption on Level Two is that there are no beginnings and endings, only cycles and transitions. Life on Level Two is a spiral of cyclic activity within which our lives can remain stable for long periods, then can change quite rapidly when energy flows into and out of the spiral. It's within this dynamic of stability and change, expansion and contraction, ebb and flow, that the Mysterious Source is manifested into individual form and experience.

It's a law of thermodynamics that energy can neither be created nor destroyed, although it can shift to a new state. This reveals that energy is immortal, a quality that could also be ascribed to our energy body. Understanding this allows us to comprehend with absolute surety the truth of reincarnation. The death experience only occurs for the physical body on Level One.

The third assumption on Level Two is that time is synchronous. This means that our experiences on Level Two are outside of the time-space continuum, and that all time is now. This also implies that everything that has ever happened, as well as everything that *will* happen, is all going on at once, interconnected though the matrix of the *aka* field. This is how past and future lives can be perceived and connected with. This is the manner in which psychics and shamans can uncover something that happened in the past, even generations ago. This is how shamans may even travel across time.

All energy medicine, including Reiki, qigong, energy balancing and transfer, as well as the psychotherapeutic healing modalities and several shamanic techniques to be discussed shortly, take place on Level Two. Acupuncture and acupressure are performed on Level One, but are experienced on Level Two.

Level Three: This is where we find the spiritual worlds, the *Dreamtime* of the Australian Aborigines, the *Other Worlds* of the Celts, and the *Po* of the Polynesians. Level Three is often referred to simply as *The Sacred,* and it's the *astral* level in which our personal oversoul lives as an immortal being of pure energy rather than as form.

This is the plane of realization, in which there's nothing to gain and nothing to experience. Spiritual consciousness makes the knower, knowing, and the known, one. It's in this manner that perception, knowledge, and action can occur simultaneously; and like Level Two, all space is here and all time is now.

The great three-leveled world system of *non-ordinary* reality is located here—those beautiful, awesome regions in which the shaman journeys to connect with the spirits, as well as with the power that the spirits possess. These "worlds" appear to exist in layers, with the various levels distinguished by their density, as well as by who and what may be found within them. In the West, they're commonly known as the Upper Worlds, the Middle Worlds, and the Lower Worlds.

Right in the center of the stack are the Middle Worlds of human dreaming—the same mysterious realms where we go at night when we're asleep. This is also where we find ourselves right after the death experience—the post-mortem Bardo states of the Tibetans, and the purgatory of Judeo-Christianity—regions populated largely by the souls of recently deceased humans. Everything that has a physical aspect on Level One seems to have a dream aspect in the Middle Worlds of Level Three, which is why many refer to the physical world as the Middle World. Our sacred garden, to be discussed shortly, is usually found in the dreams on this level.

Below them, we find the Lower Worlds, formed by the collective dreaming of nature. This is where the shaman journeys to connect with the spirits who are part of nature—with the spirit of wolf, bear, raven, tiger, eagle, or deer; with the spirit of oak, corn, or healing herb; and even with the elementals—the spirit of fire, water, earth, or stone. Shamans and mystics of all traditions across time have discovered that many of these spirits are willing to come into relationship with humans as spirit helpers, providing us with protection and support, and by association, with the power that they possess.

Above the Middle Worlds, in turn, are the Upper Worlds, formed by the collective dreaming of the gods and goddesses and the angelic forces, as well as the spiritual heroes and heroines of the past. It is within these luminous, light-filled regions that we may find connection with our spirit guides and ascended masters, as well as the members of our council of elder spirits. Many of the beings who exist in the Upper Worlds may serve us as spirit teachers, and it is among them that we have a very special connection indeed—our personal oversoul.

Interestingly, these imaginal realms are perceived in much the same way by visionaries of all cultural traditions, everywhere, implying that all human beings may be linked by a basic psychic unity, as some anthropologists and psychologists have claimed. It also suggests that these dream worlds are separate from the one who perceives them and that they have their own autonomous existence, a claim that shamans everywhere affirm with confidence.

These spirits, higher and lower, may often appear spontaneously to nontribal Westerners in psychotherapeutic sessions; and increasing numbers of therapists, using guided visualization and various hypnotherapies, are encouraging their clients to interact with and learn from these imaginal beings.[8]

The first two assumptions by which the spiritual worlds of Level Three may be experienced are (1) that everything within them is symbolic, and (2) that everything is part of a pattern. These symbols are the archetypes that are well known to mythologists, psychologists, and shamans alike, and the pattern is the great tapestry into which they're woven. The fabric of this tapestry, spread out across the continuum of Level Three, *is* the spirit world, and it's carried and maintained by the *aka* matrix in Level Two.

Needless to say, the human sector is already woven into the pattern, and we ourselves are the weavers of our part of the fabric. We accomplish this extraordinary task though our actions on Level One; through our thoughts, intentions, and emotions on Level Two; and through our dreaming on Level Three. Everything that we've become and accomplished on our long voyage across time is woven into the tapestry—everything.

Considered from this perspective, the spirit world can be thought of as a level of relativity in which space and time; galaxies and stars; and animals, plants, and humans achieve meaning only through relationship with each other.

This insight brings up the third assumption: In the level of the dream, everything means what we think it means—a statement implying that each of us must interpret our symbols, as well as our dreams, for ourselves. No one can do this for us with accuracy, because our dreams, visions, and symbols have come to us for a reason, and often from many sources. Our job is to figure them out, a task that will deepen our awareness of ourselves, as well as everything else.

The healing techniques of spirit medicine occur primarily on this level, although the energetic *aka* connections of the grid of Level Two are obviously utilized as well. We'll discuss them in the chapters that follow.

The *kahunas* say that there are actually 12 levels of reality, awareness, and experience, and so we might mention yet one more—one of great concern to most of us that exists beyond the spirit/dream worlds of Level Three. This is a dimension that's defined in different ways in different cultures, according to the belief systems that these cultures hold and express. This is the level of *The Source*.

This is the divine field that the Taoists call *Tao;* that Buddhists call *Buddha-mind;* that Hindus call *Brahma;* that Judeo-Christians call *Yaweh, Jehovah,* or *God;* that Muslims call *Allah;* that many Native Americans today refer to as *The Great Spirit;* that the Algonquins around the Great Lakes of North America call *Gitchi Manitou;* that Hawaiians call *Keave* or *I'o* or *IAO;* and that Papa Henry referred to as *Ke Akua.*

The visionary fieldwork of countless mystics and shamans across time affirms that it's not some fatherly creator god as defined by the mythologies of our monotheistic traditions. That celestial being, sitting up in heaven, listening to our prayers and working in mysterious ways, is our oversoul, our personal god-self, and it is dual-natured, possessing and expressing qualities that are both masculine *and* feminine.

Conversely, the Source is a purely subjective state, utterly remote, unfathomable, and usually unapproachable. It's the ultimate source of the power that infuses everything with life force. Shamans and visionaries affirm with absolute confidence that while it can be directly experienced, it cannot be described.[9]

The Source could also be called the *unitive field,* because on this level there's only one assumption: that everything, everywhere is an aspect of it and part of a vast, ever-expanding One-ness. On this level, there's no sense of individuation. There's only the One—and this One exists as a divine sea of grace that has no boundaries and knows no shores.

And beyond? Despite many well-intentioned claims from many organized religious traditions, no one knows if there's a Great Dreamer, an Unmoved Mover, who is the Source of the Source. This is, and will forever be, the Great Mystery.

With this foundation, we may now turn our attention toward spirit medicine, and as we do, we must keep the soul cluster in mind, as well as its relation to both the physical and energetic bodies; and how these, in turn, are placed within the three levels of reality—physical, mental-emotional-energetic, and spiritual.

This perception of how we're put together, and how we function within this composite matrix, contains the secret passage to self-realization, as well as the key to self-healing.

≋ ≋ ≋

PART II
Spirit Medicine

9

The Master Healer in the Imaginal Realms

HW: When Westerners hear the word *shaman*, most of us tend to conjure up an image of a masked and costumed tribal person dancing around a fire in the dark, involved in some strange ritual, accompanied by drumbeats. Yet within that cultural shell of mask, costume, and ritual, there's a man or woman who has a set of very real skills.

All true shamans are able to intentionally expand their conscious awareness, accessing specific *altered states* through which they achieve a direct, transpersonal connection with the spiritual worlds of Level Three. Through training, shamans deepen and stabilize this ability; and through mastery, they learn to roam freely through the mysterious multileveled geography of non-ordinary reality, where they encounter beings commonly referred to as *spirits*.

These beings may be of many different kinds—the spirits of elements, plants, and animals in the Lower Worlds, for example; or the spirits of deceased humans as well as personal ancestors in the Middle Worlds. Shamans may also connect with the spirits of ascended masters and guides, as well as angelic forces, in the Upper Worlds. It is through these relationships, higher and lower, that shamans may gain access to the power, as well as the wisdom, that these spirits possess.

This ability clearly sets shamans apart from other kinds of religious practitioners, revealing them to be both cosmic explorers on the one hand, as well as spiritual activists on the other.[10]

In the West, shamans have been largely unknown figures for much of the past 500 years, and those possessing shamanic abilities have tended to keep a relatively low profile. In traditional societies, by contrast, shamans are very well known and may hold positions of elevated social standing and political power.

Shamanic expertise tends to run in families, a fact that has led some investigators to suggest that their unusual abilities, which some might call *paranormal,* may have a genetic foundation. If true, this suggests the existence of *a program* for altering consciousness on the inner hard drive of our DNA—a program that's actually quite *normal* and that can be double-clicked by using the right "mouse."

Among the time-tested methods that have been pioneered and perfected by shamans for activating the program, the monotonous, driving rhythm of the drum and the rattle is virtually universal. Through hundreds of training workshops across the years, Jill and I have observed thousands of nontribal Westerners successfully activate this innate ability in response to the physical stimulus of the drum and the rattle . . . and often on the very first attempt!

This has led us to suspect that a substantial portion of the general human population may possess the program.[11] If true, the ability to engage in visionary experience may be part of the hereditary birthright of all human beings everywhere—both traditional peoples and nontribal moderns alike—so the knowledge contained within these chapters belongs to everyone.

Accomplished shamans, sanctified by their initiation and furnished with their guardian spirits, are holy people. They are men and women who often become master healers, able to perform on the physical, mental-emotional-energetic, and spiritual levels of being. Spirit medicine is most definitely their specialty area, however, for it's in the imaginal realms of Level Three that shamans are able to engage the compassionate spirits who are willing to assist us in various ways.[12]

These forces, for that's what spirits are, may help the

shaman restore power to those who've lost it, an ability known as *power augmentation*. They may also provide vital information to the shaman to be conveyed to a client, a practice known as *divination;* or they may collaborate with the shaman in repairing the holes torn in the fabric of someone's soul, a healing modality generally known as *soul retrieval.*

Through direct experience, shamans discover that most of us can learn how to draw upon these compassionate forces when we're in need. They also know that these sympathetic spirits are not all-powerful, that they need our help in opening up a bridge or channel between their reality and ours in order to be of service.

Shamans are the ones who use their bodies and minds as the bridge between the worlds. When the bridge is formed, miracles happen. And this is true magic.

≋

In summary, shamans function as medicinemakers in whose capable hands the physical and metaphysical equilibrium of their communities rest. Through their extraordinary abilities and through their willingness to be of service, shamans may bring the power of the sacred into our lives, a skill that then allows them to manifest various things—healing work, for example.

≈ ≈ ≈

10

Spirit Medicine and Physical Medicine

JK: We live in a time in which the nature and quality of health care represent major areas of concern within the national and international community. In response, our view of health care is changing, and increasing numbers of spiritual seekers and health-care providers alike are reconsidering the role that the mind—and by association, spirituality—plays in healing. In the process, society at large is becoming increasingly aware of complementary and alternative medicine, and it's precisely here that the indigenous peoples may have something vital to offer us.[13]

The traditionals make a clear distinction between physical medicine and spirit medicine, yet they view them as complementary, as two halves of a whole. It's important to make this point because many people today have had negative experiences within the Western medical system, and some dismiss physical medicine with disdain, branding it as dysfunctional or even harmful. Yet if someone were seriously injured in a car accident and bleeding internally, it's quite obvious that this wouldn't be the moment to pick up the rattle and go into trance. This would be the time for that person to find him- or herself in an operating room with a world-class surgeon, anesthesiologist, and medical team.

In the same vein, if a tribal warrior were carried into camp with an arrow sticking out of his body, this would be the moment to get the projectile out of the wound, stem the bleeding, prevent infection, and promote healing. This would be the time for physical medicine; and all shamans, in their capacity as healers, know a great deal about it.

In considering the relationship between physical medicine and spirit medicine, however, let's take a hypothetical case where an individual discovers that he or she has a life-threatening illness such as cancer.

In the standard Western medical paradigm, that person would be referred to an oncologist who would go to work with everything medically available, from chemotherapy to radiation and possibly surgery. This protocol is much in keeping with our belief that the primary purpose of the practice of medicine is the avoidance of death and the prolongation of life.

Among the indigenous peoples, however, treatment for the cancer might be quite different. Shamans know that everything in existence has a physical aspect, an energetic aspect, and a spiritual aspect. They also understand that illness gains much of its initial power, as well as its meaning, from its spiritual aspect.

Given this perception, the shaman would most likely address the illness at all three levels—physical, energetic, and spiritual. If the illness can be addressed at the spiritual level, its energetic expression will be progressively diminished, shifting the balance within the sufferer's physical body from disorder and disease toward harmony and balance—a shift that may be just the medicine required to allow the body soul, functioning as restorer, to overcome the illness.

The shaman also knows that when your soul cluster is in good shape, there are no worries. Yet if one or more of your three souls is diminished or damaged, you've got a problem. This reveals why the primary purpose of the practice of spirit medicine is to restore, nurture, and preserve the soul.

As we pass through life on the physical plane, things happen: We contract flus, colds, and bacterial infections, and we sustain physical injuries, like falling off our bikes as children or suffering sports injuries. As adults, we may throw our back out or experience a serious accident—in the process acquiring bruises, cuts, sprains, infections, lacerations, and sometimes broken bones.

Some of us may also deal with serious illnesses of an internal nature like cancer, hepatitis, heart disease, or multiple sclerosis. Eventually we pass through old age, and the progressive infirmity and death of the physical body. These are the givens—they're all to be expected as part of what it means to be an embodied, living being on Level One. But these are all *effects,* and what the shaman is primarily interested in is the *cause.*

In looking through the shamanic healer's eyes, the ultimate causes of virtually all illness are to be found within the imaginal realms of Level Three—in those same regions from which illness derives its initial power to affect us adversely. Because of this, it's not enough to simply suppress the *effects* of illness with medication on the physical plane and hope for the best. For true healing to occur, the *causes* of the illness must be addressed.

From the shaman's perspective, there are three classic causes of illness, and interestingly, they're not microbes or bacteria or viruses. Rather, they're negative internal states that appear within us in response to negative or traumatic life experiences. The first among these is *disharmony.*

11

Disharmony

DISHARMONY is what we experience when life suddenly loses its meaning or when we've lost an important connection to our lives.

Let's take the case of an elderly couple who've been married for a long time, and suddenly one of them dies. They may not have had a perfect relationship, yet there's a deep bond between them because of all they've shared. The survivor may go into crisis upon the loss of his or her mate, and within a short time, he or she may come down with something medically challenging, like cancer. Suddenly, they're gone, too.

That's disharmony.

Disharmony may also result from the sudden loss of our identity, our sense of "belonging to." Let's take the case of a high-level corporate executive, a woman in her early 50s who's at the top of her field. One day, the management executives in her corporation decide to hire someone right out of business school for a third of her salary, so they terminate her employment sooner than expected. Now what do you think her chances are of getting rehired at the same level in her profession? Remember, she's just been fired.

Six months later, she's still looking for work and is in a deep state of disharmony. Her debts are mounting and she suspects (rightly) that she's lost her livelihood and that she's going to have to start over. One day, she finds a lump in her breast and goes to her doctor, who does a biopsy and gives her the grim diagnosis.

Now, without making any claims, could it be that the cause of her breast cancer is in some way involved with losing her job?

The state of disharmony that we experience in response to such life situations causes a diminishment of our personal power. This can happen in a subtle manner on the one hand, or in a catastrophic, life-shaking way on the other. When we experience disempowerment, or "power loss," it affects our energetic matrix, rendering us vulnerable to illness.

≋ ≋ ≋

12

Fear

THE second classic cause of illness is *fear*. People who are walking around with a chronic sense of fear gnawing away at them are doubly vulnerable to illness because their anxiety aggressively and progressively diminishes their sense of well-being, and this, in turn, affects their feeling of being safe in the world.

This sense of well-being is the base upon which our personal health system stands. When this foundation is affected negatively, it diminishes the ability of our immune system to function. And when our immune system goes down, we're in trouble.

It's not too difficult to see that there's a feedback mechanism at work here. Fear, and the anxiety it creates, produces disharmony. In the same breath, disharmony generates fear, and if the two of them are working together, it doubly affects the protective mantle of the body's immune system, as well as the energetic matrix. Illness is the inevitable result.

It's no surprise to Western medical practitioners that disharmony and fear can manifest themselves in diseases that are recognizable to science. Almost 500 years ago, the Renaissance physician Paracelsus observed that "the fear of disease is more dangerous than the disease itself."

But suppose an individual with a serious, life-threatening illness lacks fear entirely? Here's a rather thought-provoking example.

In the recent past, medical doctors believed that the mortality rate for AIDS sufferers was 100 percent—that if you contracted the HIV virus, then you would be resigned to a death sentence. It was just a matter of time.

However, an AIDS-related study published in the *New England Journal of Medicine* has revealed something quite extraordinary. Researchers at the UCLA School of Medicine have reported unambiguous evidence of an infant boy who twice tested positive for the HIV virus, once at 19 days of age and again one month later. But when this child was tested again as a kindergartener at age five, he was HIV negative.

The virus was not lying dormant, awaiting some external cue to become active. It had been eliminated from his body, *and the child appeared to have been HIV-free for at least four years.*[14]

Could it be that the immune system of this infant, completely ignorant of the fact that he had a terminal illness, remained strong? Could it be that his body soul, lacking the fear and other negative emotions that the awareness of having this "deadly disease" would ordinarily generate in an older individual, simply went to work as it was pro-grammed to do and killed the virus in the first year of his life?

There's also another possibility here, one that regu-larly escapes the notice of the scientific community. This brings us to consider the third classic cause of illness—the phenomenon known to indigenous healers as *soul loss*.

≋ ≋ ≋

13
Soul Loss

JK: Among the traditionals, soul loss is regarded as *the* most serious diagnosis and *the* major cause of premature death and serious illness, yet curiously, it's not even mentioned in our Western medical textbooks. The closest acknowledged context is that "he/she has lost the will to live."

In Western society, soul loss is most easily understood as damage to a person's life essence, a phenomenon that usually occurs in response to trauma. When the trauma is severe, this may result in a fragmentation of that person's soul cluster, with the shattered soul parts dissociating, fleeing an intolerable situation. In overwhelming circumstances, these soul parts may not return.

The causes of soul loss can be many and varied. There may be traumatic perinatal issues that occur around children's birth experiences, such as arriving into life only to discover that they're not wanted or that they're the wrong gender—they've come in as a girl when everyone was hoping for a boy. Soul loss can also occur when a child is mercilessly bullied or teased at home or at school, day after day, or when young people are molested by those who are supposed to be caring for them. When someone has been raped or assaulted; has suffered a shocking betrayal, a bitter divorce, a traumatic abortion, a terrible car accident, or even a serious surgery, soul loss is assured.

Many of the young men and women who were sent to war in Iraq, Kuwait, Vietnam, and beyond came home personally damaged because they had suffered terrible soul loss. Our medical specialists labeled their disorders as *post-traumatic stress disorder,* but they had little initially to offer these "walking wounded" in terms of true healing, and many who survived are still deeply traumatized at the soul level by what happened to them in battle.

Soul loss is easily recognizable if you know what you're looking for. Here is a checklist of some of the classic symptoms:

- Feelings of being fragmented,
  of not being all here
- Blocked memory—an inability to remember
  parts of one's life
- Being unable to feel love or receive love
  from another
- Emotional remoteness
- A sudden onset of apathy or listlessness
- A lack of initiative, enthusiasm, or joy
- A failure to thrive
- An inability to make decisions
  or discriminate

- Chronic negativity
- Addictions
- Suicidal tendencies
- Melancholy or despair
- Chronic depression

Perhaps the most common symptom of soul loss is depression. According to a 2003 Harvard Medical School Study published in the *Journal of the American Medical Association,* between 13 and 14 million American adults suffer from a major depressive episode in a given year, representing nearly 5 percent of the total population, and sometimes that number jumps in response to a national trauma. On the Friday following 9/11, a television newscast revealed that seven out of ten Americans polled were experiencing significant depression in response to the tragedy, an indicator of soul loss on a national scale.

Although the term *soul loss* is not familiar to most Westerners, examples of it are expressed daily in our language and descriptions of personal hardships. Media interviews and news reports include individuals' comments such as "I lost a part of myself when that (trauma) happened" and "I have not been the same since." When discussing soul loss with a number of individuals, I found that almost everyone had a sense of having lost a "part" of themselves at some time in life, yet virtually no one had the awareness that the missing part(s) could be recovered.

They can.

14
Illness Intrusions

HW: When we're diminished by disharmony, when our soul cluster has taken a major hit, or when we're in a state of stress, anxiety, or fear, we become vulnerable to intrusions entering our personal energetic field. When the intrusions are strong enough, they may take up residence, distorting the pattern of our matrix and producing the symptoms recognizable as illness.

In spirit medicine, illness is caused by intrusions—by something that comes into us from without. It could be a virus, a bacterium, an arrow, or a negative thoughtform. However, from the shaman's perspective, the illness intrusion is not the primary issue. The real problem is the diminishment of our personal power or the holes torn in the fabric of our soul that allowed the intrusion to enter in the first place.

Negative thoughts, feelings, and intentions can be directed toward us like spiritual poison darts by those who hold us in disregard—an old lover or spouse who just can't let go, a hostile neighbor who spews forth profanity at us, in-laws who find us unworthy, or a jealous sibling or co-worker who simply despises us. When this is done with outright malice, it forms the *modus operandi* of negative witchcraft and sorcery. The Yoruba people of West Africa call it *juju.*

When the negative thoughtforms become frequent, generated by another's anger toward us, for example, they take on density, continually fueled by the heightened emotions of the sender. Our body soul immediately picks them up. Remember, the body soul is the perceiver of that which can be seen, as well as that which is unseen. It notices everything, even those things that we're not consciously aware of.

If our soul cluster is in good shape, these negative intentions may simply bounce off or pass through, allowing us to continue much as before. If our soul cluster is damaged or our power is down, however, the negativity and the anger can be internalized, taking up residence within us as an intrusion and disrupting our sense of well-being. Over time, this may cause an increasing sense of dis-ease, which, in turn, causes a progressive diminishment of our life force.

Individuals may also create their own intrusions through an ongoing preoccupation with the negative. Medical intuitive Caroline Myss describes them as *energy circuits* held within a person's matrix—knots of coherence that can continually draw from the body's daily supply of power. Often, these energy circuits represent unfinished emotional business that we're carrying around like baggage. As our body soul (subconsciously) or our mental soul (consciously) focuses on these negative thoughts or memories, the flow of energy toward them is increased, and they expand, diminishing us on the energetic level even more.

Such well-established intrusions may accumulate over time, building up a presence within us much like the clutter that grows in our living space year after year, including all the stuff we inherited from our parents that we're not quite ready to let go of yet. It is then that an unexpected trauma may suddenly tip the scale from balance into disharmony, from ease into disease . . . with the inevitable result: illness.

≋

In summary, the energy body is very responsive to thoughts and emotions. Negative memories, reflections, ruminations, sentiments, or feelings that are held for any length of time within the energy body may form intrusions that will distort the pattern of our energetic matrix. Since the structure, as well as the functioning, of the physical body is determined by this energetic pattern, distortions in one will bring about distortions in the other. And once the pattern of the matrix is distorted, the body soul can no longer function effectively as the inner healer.

Remember, the body soul is not creative. It needs that energetic blueprint in order to make repairs.

The *kahuna* healers of Hawai'i paid great attention to learning how to direct their thoughts. They knew that through focused concentration, they could help restore the energy body to an undistorted state, and this, in turn, could facilitate the return of harmony and balance in the physical aspect.

One of the last publicly practicing *kahunas*, David Kaonohiokala Bray (1889–1968), dispelled the negative thoughtforms of his clients by first leading them toward increased self-awareness. The source of the thoughtforms was then sought out, revealing how they functioned as well as why the client would continue to hold on to them.

The goal was to help clients release the negative, allowing them to choose another attitude and a new way for being in the world.[15]

Through dialogue, as well as his own expanded awareness, Daddy Bray, as he was known, analyzed the thoughtforms of his client, especially those created by distorted emotions and thoughts during chronic mental poisoning. He knew that these negative thoughtforms could become so dense that they might actually appear as separate beings—as the demons, dark forces, and evil spirits so prevalent in the world's mythologies.

In the same breath, he understood that once these thoughtforms achieved a certain density, they could act as psychic-energetic "vampires," literally feeding on the client's fears and drawing energy directly from their vitality. It's possible that many of the documented cases of spirit possession and so-called spirit attachments may actually fall into this category.

The *kahuna's* task is to expose the thoughtforms for what they really are—unreal demons or phantoms that have no existence in themselves, and which cease to exist once released by the sufferer. If the client continues to feed them, they hang around. But when the sufferer no longer gives them what they want, they're history.

≈ ≈ ≈

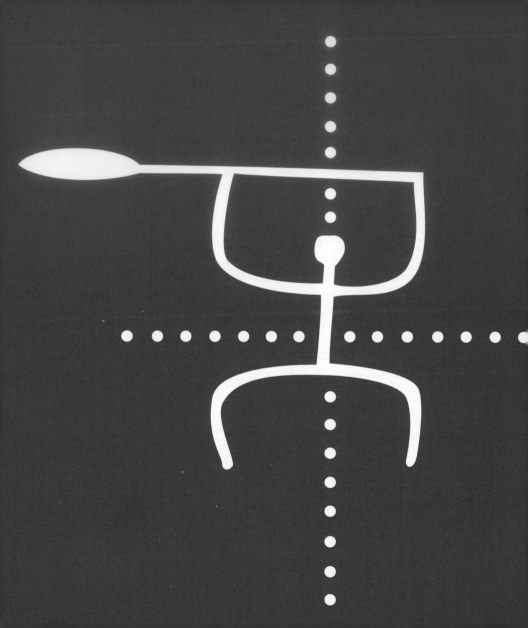

15
Power Augmentation

HW: Healing in spirit medicine typically occurs in successive stages. The first might be called *power augmentation*, a process in which the shaman enhances his or her client's power supply quickly and dramatically.

One of the most effective ways of doing this is to bring the client into relationship with a spirit helper. To accomplish this, the shamanic healer typically journeys into the dream world with that intention—to find a spirit who will provide the client with power, protection, and support. The frequency with which these helping spirits appear as favorite animals, or as animal-human composites, has given rise to the term *power animal*.

The helper could just as easily appear as the spirit of a favorite plant, herb, or tree. It might approach as a wise teacher or angelic being; or it might even be the spirit of a deceased ancestor who's compassionately concerned for the sufferer—maybe a grandparent who's already passed over. The shaman's job is to find this spirit and persuade it to come into relationship so that it can channel energy in a healing capacity to the one suffering.

Simply knowing that a spirit has come into partnership with you, one that has your well-being at heart, is extraordinarily empowering, especially if you learn how to make contact with this entity by utilizing the shamanic method yourself.

The spirit helper might also come to you as an old indigenous medicine man or woman. The frequency with which the spirits of Native Americans come into relationship with Westerners is quite striking. It seems that these wise beings are less interested in ethnicity and are more concerned with being of service to the one whose heart is open.

It's equally as possible, of course, that an oversoul, whose essence is currently residing in an Anglo, African, or Asian body this time around, existed in many Indian bodies in the past. If true, this suggests why so many are drawn toward the worldviews and rituals of cultures other than their own. (More information on personal empowerment may be found in Chapter 24.)

≋ ≋ ≋

16
Diagnosis

JK: The next level of healing in spirit medicine involves the correct *diagnosis* of the problem, and this can be accomplished in different ways.

Shamanic healers may go into trance and connect with their spirit helpers to ask for information about the nature of the client's illness—a practice known as *divination*. All shamans proclaim with authority that they receive information from the spirits in this way that they couldn't access on their own.

This "data" may then be confirmed by another exercise in which spirit-medicine practitioners literally journey into a client's body. This is done with permission—always—and once within their client's field, they look for the intrusions that don't belong there. These intrusions most often appear in a symbolic form that the shaman finds repulsive—as maggots in a person's liver, for example, symbolizing liver dysfunction; or as scorpions in their intestines, revealing the presence of irritable bowel syndrome, perhaps.

There are also those with the gift of true psychic sight who can utilize clairvoyance to perceive the energy body on Level Two quite clearly, as well as the intrusions embedded within it. This ability to do so is well known to traditional peoples and involves using what Australian Aborigines call the "strong eye," or what the Hawaiians would call *maka 'ike,* the eye of spiritual wisdom. Others say they see through the heart.

Spirit-medicine practitioners may also confirm the presence of intrusions by running their hands through the client's energetic field a few inches above and around the physical body, and their body soul may experience an empathic emotional response. The intrusions can usually be felt as abnormally cool or hot places, or as a "breeze" that seems to be blowing out of the body. Traditional people sometimes run a loosely held feather through the person's field, carefully observing how it responds, lifting up here or dipping down there.

These ways of perceiving illness can be enormously enhanced by asking helping spirits for assistance, a practice that distinguishes spirit medicine from straight energy medicine. In response, healers may suddenly find their hands moved involuntarily to a particular area of the client's body, while information may arrive within their mind in a symbolic format.

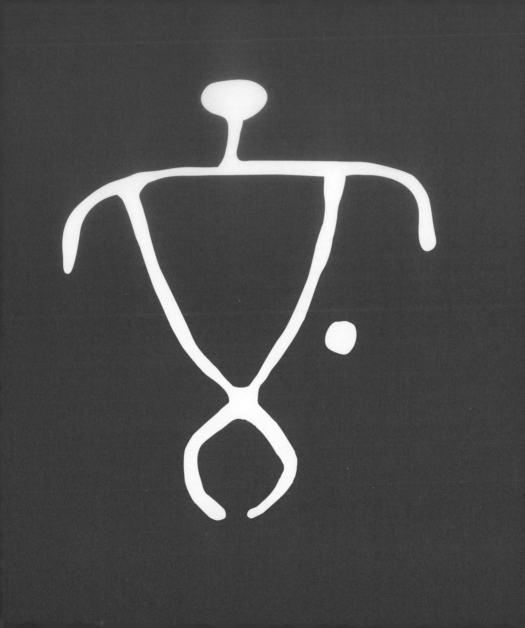

17
Extraction

HW: Once the shamanic practitioner has a clear view of the intrusions, the third stage in the healing process involves *extracting* them from the client's body. This is easiest to do while in the expanded state of awareness and while still in connection with one's spirits.

Traditional shamans collect spiritual helpers because the more they have working with them, the more they can accomplish. These spirits possess qualities and abilities that distinguish them from each other. Some are good at providing protection, while others are specialists who provide power or information. Some are superb at healing work, which is why most medicinemakers have one or more healing masters working with them.[16]

It's interesting to note that virtually all shamans, in every culture, claim that it's the spirits who do the work at their request, not themselves. Shamans and their spirits thus work as a team, in tandem, with the healer functioning as the bridge between the transpersonal and the physical realms.

In doing extraction work, shamans may invite a power animal or healing master to help them or even merge with them, a practice known as *trance-mediumship*. Then, with the spirit working with or through them, they may use their mouth to literally suck the intrusion out of the person's body. Sometimes, they'll place an object in their mouth, such as a crystal or a piece of meat, to serve as a trap to catch the illness when it comes out. But just as often, the hands are used to do the extraction.

The question, of course, now comes up: Is the shaman really extracting something from the client, energetic or otherwise, or is it the patient's belief system that goes to work, activating the well-known placebo effect in response to the healing ritual?

Shamans claim with the authority of long practice that they do indeed extract something from the client, specifically the illness's energetic essence. In the same breath, it's also clear that the presence of a power-filled shamanic healer with a proven track record for curing people can also play a pivotal role, activating that well-known healing response called *placebo*. If sufferers have confidence that the healer will cure them, they usually get better. If they have no confidence, then this is their problem.

But sometimes the magic works anyway, with or without the input of the one afflicted. Many years ago, I developed a severe case of tendonitis in my left shoulder and could not raise my arm without extreme pain. One day, almost two years after the condition first appeared, I exacerbated it to the point where I had to put my arm in a sling.

I went to an orthopedist and got an x-ray, and there was the intrusion, or maybe we should call it a distortion—a large calcium crystal in my left supraspinatus tendon, the one that originates from the muscle nestled on top of the shoulder blade and then runs across the shoulder joint and inserts into the humerus, the upper arm bone, enabling the raising of the arm.

About a month later, I was at a shamanic training workshop where I felt drawn to ask a young woman if she would do an extraction on my shoulder. She agreed to try. In the ritual that followed, she went into deep trance and connected with one of her spirits. She then worked on my shoulder for what seemed like half an hour, using her fingers like probes, gently working invisible objects down the length of my arm before pulling them out of my fingers.

When the workshop came to an end, I didn't feel any particular relief, and I drove home with my shoulder still tender—but the situation shifted markedly within the next few days. Within a week, I could raise my arm above my shoulder, and within three weeks, the pain was completely gone.

Now, conditions like tendonitis tend to come and go, and it's not really necessary to claim that anything paranormal happened. Yet it's of interest that the issue resolved itself within those days immediately following the extraction ritual. My tendonitis has not returned.

≋ ≋ ≋

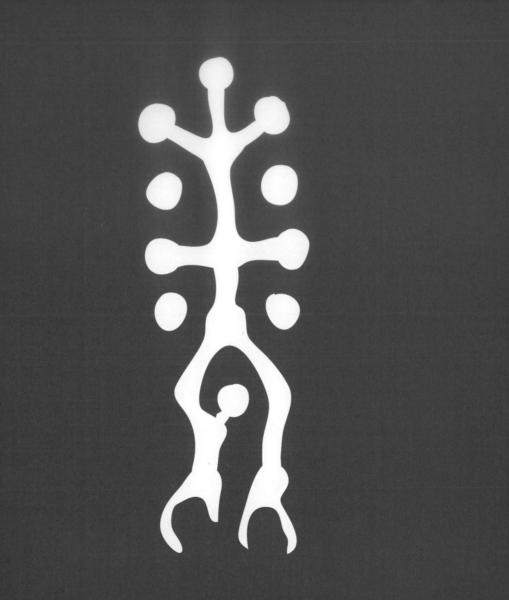

18

Soul Retrieval

JK: Soul retrieval is the definitive healing modality in spirit medicine because it affords a reunion of dissociated soul part(s) with the person's life essence, thereby allowing individuals to have more of themselves available to live their lives in the present moment.

Soul retrieval affords a reconstitution, repairing the holes torn in the fabric of the soul cluster. But how does the process of soul retrieval actually work?

All of us, in every culture everywhere, had ancestors who were hunters if we go back far enough. In doing soul-retrieval work, shamanic practitioners team up with the spirits who assist them, then they go to work together, tracking the lost soul parts like hunters.

And this is where spirit medicine has something important to offer the psychotherapeutic paradigm. Psychologists and psychiatrists know about dissociation, but where do the dissociated parts go? In doing soul retrieval, shamanic healers and their spiritual assistants locate the lost soul parts in the Lower, Middle, or Upper Worlds of Level Three. There they enter into relationship with them, convincing them to return and bringing them back to their original owner. In this process, the person's soul cluster is restored, and their energetic matrix in Level Two may return to its former undistorted state.

Interestingly, a soul part that has taken refuge in the Lower Worlds may often be found in the company of an animal spirit who's caring for it. When this soul part is brought back, the animal spirit may return with it, resulting in what is called a *power-animal retrieval.*

A soul part located in the Middle Worlds of dream may be found in the company of an ancestor, perhaps a revered grandparent who has already crossed over. A soul part in the Upper Worlds may be seeking reconnection with its oversoul, a guardian angel, or even with its "soul family."

As the soul cluster is restored, the shaman instructs the client in how to take an active role in reintegrating these lost self-aspects, assuring a successful reunion and ensuring that the extracted illness intrusions will not recur.

In traditional societies like those of the Pacific Northwest, soul-retrieval specialists were often known as *soul catchers.* The traditionals used to say that real soul catchers only appear every hundred years or so, implying that not all shamanic practitioners are proficient at soul retrieval.

I discovered quite by accident that I'm a soul catcher. Originally I was trained as a physical therapist, and for the past 25 years or so, I've worked in acute-care rehabilitation as well as home health. I'm now in private practice, specializing almost entirely in soul-retrieval work, guided by my spirits who also facilitate power augmentation and divination work. Although I trained with several teachers accomplished in soul retrieval to acquire the basic tools, the heart of my method was taught to me by my spirit helpers, quite clearly revealing their pivotal role as teachers and guides in the practice of spirit medicine.

Early on in my practice, a young woman in her early 20s made contact with me. She was active, athletic, and accomplished in kayaking. As one of Hank's former students, she was aware of the phenomenon of soul loss and had gotten in touch with me because she suspected she was suffering from it. In talking with her, I learned that she had recently had a close call while filming a kayaking documentary. As she coursed over a waterfall, she suddenly lost control of her craft and was pinned upside down in her kayak on the bottom of a pool. As the minutes ticked by, she was trapped by the force of the water falling directly onto her kayak from above. While frantically applying her skills to free herself, she reported being aware that it would take considerable luck for her to survive.

Fortunately, she managed to extract herself from her craft and pop to the surface before she drowned, yet during the following week, she found herself descending into an uncharacteristic, ever-deepening depression. Rather than jumping for joy about being alive, she was losing interest in all things meaningful to her, including her film project.

While doing the soul-retrieval journey that she requested, I discovered that a portion of her soul was still in the pool below the waterfall, still struggling to survive and much in need of a reunion with her. This soul return was accomplished through the efforts of my team of spirits who work with me, creating an opportunity for the soul part to be bridged back to her.

The kayaker reported feeling an immediate shift, and the oppressive depression that had gripped her was resolved within days. She then went on to complete her film project and to make other life-affirming changes as well.

In summary, it can be seen that the primary causes of illness only become a threat when a person's natural protective mantle develops a weakness. When these classic causes—disharmony, fear, and soul loss—manifest themselves as physical or psychological symptoms, they must be dealt with at the energetic and spiritual levels for true healing to occur.

The perspective of spirit medicine is still quite foreign to most of our Western health-care practitioners, doctors, nurses, and therapists alike. However, this worldview, so familiar to the indigenous peoples, is gaining wider acceptance . . . because it greatly assists in the healing process, and because it works.

The shaman's talents, like those of the Western-trained physician, lie in diagnosis—in the discovery of the identity and the nature of illness. But unlike our modern Western doctors, shamans can also empower their clients dramatically, divine the ultimate cause of an illness while in an expanded state of awareness, neutralize them at their spiritual and energetic levels, and prevent their recurrence by utilizing the assistance of compassionate forces poised to help us just beyond the borders of this physical world we all take so much for granted.

PART III
Healing in the Garden

19

How to Use
the Compact Disc

HW: The CD that accompanies this book contains a single hour-long track of steady, monotonous rhythm, combining both drumming and rattling. When this powerful physical stimulus is accompanied by a focused command from the mental soul to open that inner doorway, the body soul responds, enabling us to journey into the ordinarily hidden worlds of Level Three, where we may enlist the aid of our helping spirits and master healers, inviting them to do work on our behalf or for others.

The steady, rhythmic sound is the "mouse" that double-clicks our program, allowing our consciousness to expand. The ability to do this is a learned skill that improves with practice. If at first you don't seem to succeed, continue trying. Once your body soul gets what it is that you're after, you'll most likely achieve marked success.

The visionary mode of Level Three is most easily accessed while physically relaxed—preferably lying down—with the eyes covered or closed. But it can also be done while sitting comfortably in a chair or on a meditation cushion, or even propped against a stone or a tree in your own backyard.

Then again, some of us like to dance our journeys. Accordingly, the tempo of the drumming and rattling on the CD is slower than the one that accompanies my previous book, *The Journey to the Sacred Garden,* and has been chosen specifically to facilitate your "healing dance." You can do this when home alone, or the CD can be played on a big sound system for a group involved in a healing ritual.

Those who prefer a faster tempo may use the CD that accompanies *The Journey to the Sacred Garden,* which includes two 30-minute tracks: one of the drum and one of the rattle. Whichever you select, the sound will assist you in intentionally shifting the focus of your conscious awareness into the spiritual realms where many things become possible. The rhythm will carry you into the spirit worlds, and it will bring you back again. As long as you can hear the sound, you'll never get lost.

With continued practice, you'll find that the inner doorway located within the body soul will obligingly open, and your destination will be achieved. At the end of the journey, you'll hear a shift in tempo from the slower, monotonous beat into several minutes of more rapid percussion. This is the cue to return your primary focus to your physical body. When you hear it, simply take leave of the visionary realms, and intentionally redirect your awareness back to ordinary reality.

Before using the CD, choose a time when you can be alone in your living space or wherever you are—a time when you're not tired or inclined to go to sleep.

Set your intentions in advance by thinking about where you want to go and what you want to accomplish. Then, when the time comes, simply lie down or sit comfortably, place the CD in the player, or put on your headphones (adjusting the sound to a comfortable level), and close or cover your eyes.

During the journey itself, simply remain in a suspended, relaxed state, allowing the steady resonance of the rattle and the drum to help maintain your focus "there." When you hear the "call back," shift your conscious awareness back to your physical body "here."

Try to minimize distractions by turning off your cell phone and by taking your home phone off the hook so that your journey will not be interrupted in midstream. When the journey is completed and the CD track has come to the end, emerge from the expanded state. Then spend as much time as is needed thoughtfully reviewing everything that was perceived during the exercise, making written notes to ensure that you won't forget what transpired.

Reviewing and note-taking are most important, as they are the keys to uncovering the subtleties and nuances within the greater picture that the journey is providing to you. If at first you don't seem to be getting much, try again. Shamanic journeywork is a learned skill that improves with practice.

20
Protection

HW: When we enter the spirit world, it's wise to create a perimeter of protection around our traveling selves. This can be accomplished with a short prayer (a request formed by the mental soul and directed to the oversoul) combined with a visualization (perceived as real by the body soul).

Prayer is a highly effective way to talk to "the gods." It may be as simple as directing your attention up toward your oversoul and asking for your vibrations to be set on high so that no one of equal or lesser vibration can get into your field and mess with you. Although you (here) may not fully understand what "adjusting your vibrational level to high" means, your oversoul (you there) knows exactly what this entails. And since it's in connection with you throughout your entire lifetime, your journey will take place within a sphere of protection, extended toward you from the one above who's always and forever compassionately concerned for you.

My protection prayer to my oversoul goes something like this:

> "I offer my heartfelt greetings to my utterly trustworthy ancestral spirit, my immortal oversoul that hovers over me. I also extend my greetings to the members of my council of elder teachers. I request that you provide me with power,

protection, and support as I engage in spiritual fieldwork. I also ask that my vibrations be set on high, allowing my traveling soul to journey into the spiritual realms in complete safety, while my physical body awaits my return surrounded by a perimeter of protection. I offer my profound gratitude, as well as my respect, in advance. . . ."

Some of us also like to enhance our sense of spiritual protection with a visualization, such as surrounding our journeying self in a bubble of white light or in a blue egg, or as seeing ourselves held within the hands or wings of our guardian angel. Of course, once you're in connection with your spirit helpers, you may simply turn your attention in their direction and ask them for protection, power, and support. And rest assured, it's yours for the asking.

Having performed this simple protection ritual, know with complete assurance that you'll be safe. This is most important because, as Papa Henry observed, healing work cannot be done in a state of fear.

When I engage in this ritual, I take a couple of clearing breaths, relax into the sound of the drums and the rattles, and off I go.

21
The Journey

SHAMANIC journeywork is the ancestral pre-cursor of today's guided visualizations, hypnotherapies, and guided-imagery modalities, in which the therapist is verbally directing you through the experience by suggesting where to go or what to see or do.

With journeywork, however, you're in control of the process from start to finish, creating your own objectives at the beginning—your own goals for the journey—then allowing the vision to unfold on its own, providing you with information that you're perceiving, yet not creating.

When your body soul opens that portal within it, you're venturing into the inner worlds autonomously, as a visionary explorer, supported by the vibration of the rattle or the drum. In doing so, you're engaging in an ancient human experience—the ability to vision. And once your body soul has been conditioned to do this, you may be simply stunned by the elegant simplicity, as well as the power, of this time-tested method.

There are different ways of perceiving, however. Some of us don't get those big-time visuals while in journey mode. Some receive information through the auditory channel and may hear a voice or a sound, perhaps a "tone-poem" of beautiful, tranquil music, in which information suddenly becomes available to us.

Some of us are somatic in the way we access—we just know things, as though the information is coming to us through our body. Many psychics and clairsentients fall into this category, feeling and sensing their journeys rather than seeing them. Such inner travelers may tap in to a pervading sense of tranquility or peacefulness, and while in this state, they may simply receive information in response to their need to know.

The key word is *trust*—an absolute knowing that you're safe and that you're perceiving something real, something separate from yourself that you're not making up. Remember, the body soul is the perceiver, but it's not creative. It's incapable of making anything up. It can only tell you what it has seen and what it remembers.

≋ ≋ ≋

22

The Sacred Garden

ALL of us have fond memories of locales we've been to in life, settings where we've felt complete, at peace, and at ease. Often these are places in nature where we feel a strong sense of connection. In our meditations or in our daydreaming, we often spontaneously revisit such places by simply remembering them and by recalling what it was like to be there.

Our feelings for those places, generated and sustained by the body soul, are the links that activate the *aka* connections between us here in Level One and the spiritual aspects of those settings in the dreamworlds of Level Three. Shamanic journeywork allows us to intentionally travel along these *aka* cords and enter into the "dreaming" of such places so that we may utilize them as "sacred gardens" where various tasks may then be accomplished.

Your garden might be a locality in the everyday world that you already know and love, a place where you like to go camping or walking, or even your own backyard. It can also be a purely imaginal place that you create for yourself, one that you can simply dream into existence by using your intentions and your creative imagination. Many of us did this spontaneously as children, creating an inner place that sustained and nurtured us, like Dorothy's *Oz,* Peter Pan's *Neverland,* or Alice's *Wonderland.*

As your inner explorations bring your garden into increasingly sharper focus, you will discover, as have countless others before you, that it operates by four primary rules.

1. Everything in your garden is symbolic of some aspect of you or your life experience.
   - You are on the Third Level, and this is the level of archetypes.

2. Everything in the garden can be communicated with, enhancing your understanding of both yourself and your life experiences.
   - This is called *divination*. You can talk with all the elements that make up your garden, and you'll understand what they have to say, but you must first learn to listen.

3. Everything in the garden can be changed by doing gardenwork.
   - You can make it just the way you want it to be, but first, you must master your emotions.

4. When you change your garden, some aspect of you or your life experience will shift in response.
    *   This is true magic.

≋ ≋ ≋

23
Gardenwork

THE discovery that we can do gardenwork—that is, changing or altering our sacred garden to suit ourselves—has life-changing implications.

You might wish to enhance your sacred place with a bed of sunflowers or a circle of standing stones, a waterfall to sit beside or rainbows to delight the eye. Your mental soul can simply use its power of creative imagination to conjure them into existence in your garden, and they will be there from that moment forward. To be in a place of great beauty is very uplifting and may be deeply restorative to all three levels of your being—physical, mental-emotional, and spiritual. Your garden, by its very existence, will serve you as a personal place of refuge from your everyday routine.

Remember, the body soul takes everything literally. It doesn't distinguish between reality and illusion. Your body soul perceives your garden as real.

Conversely, you might find something in your garden that you don't want there. The first rule reveals that this *something* is symbolic of some aspect of you or your life, while the third rule states that you can change it or even remove it from your garden. If that something is symbolic of an illness, the fourth rule affirms that when you diminish it or remove its spiritual aspect from your garden, you can affect its energetic aspect and extract it from your physical body.

Remember, when you change the symbols, the archetypes, of your inner reality, something within you or your outer world will change in response.

This is what magic really is.

24
The Place of Power

YOU may invite your spirit helpers, as well as your spirit teachers, to meet with you in your garden from time to time to accomplish various things. The more power you have, the easier this is to do, and the garden is a place where you may connect with power—big time.

The indigenous peoples know that this power is everywhere and in everything. They understand that it's highly dispersed throughout the universe, that it can be densely concentrated in certain places and objects, and that it infuses and animates all living beings with life force.

Accordingly, shamans and medicine people pay particular attention to maintaining and even increasing their personal supply of power because the effectiveness of all their practices is dependent on its presence as well as its "density." One's emotional state, mental attitudes, and personal behavior can also affect its ebb and flow, its abundance or its scarcity.

This power is analogous to the *mana* of the Polynesians, the *chi* of the Chinese, the *ki* of the Koreans and Japanese, the *prana* of the Hindus, the *ashe* of Santería, the *num* of the Kalahari bushmen, and the *Force* of Obi-Wan Kenobi. It's probable that all people everywhere, in every culture, have a well-developed sense of it.

In Hawai'i, the main channel through which this energy becomes available to us is the *aumakua,* our personal oversoul—our porthole into the overarching field of the human spirit, which is, in turn, in connection with the Source.

There are also, of course, the fields and currents of power that exist naturally within the physical environment, immediate sources that we can connect with through our body soul, directed by the intentionality and focused concentration of our mental soul.

The traditional peoples know with absolute certainty that this power is real—that it may be transmitted by touch, that it can be absorbed through proximity, and that it may be harnessed for positive or negative purposes, depending on the intentions of the one who can accumulate, manipulate, and focus it.

They also know that anyone can learn to connect with this power, and that through practice, each of us can learn to use this force to manifest something—such as healing, for example.

Before you use your sacred garden as a place of healing, it would be wise to build up your personal supply of power. This can be accomplished by doing a breathing exercise accompanied by an intention, a physical stimulus, and a visualization.

Your egoic mental soul is the source of your intentionality, so begin by using this self-aspect to create a strongly focused decision to connect with and take on a supercharge of energy. Holding that intention, gently shift your focus to your breathing. Breathe slowly in to the count of four, and then breathe slowly out to another four count, completely filling and emptying your lungs with each breath.

While breathing deeply, select a physical stimulus that you can do at any time and at any place, like folding your thumb into your fist and squeezing it gently. Your body soul is highly impressed by anything physical, and this small act will alert it that you mean business. It will also cue the body soul to start pulling in energy with each breath (the intention), and since this self-aspect is the interface between you and "the force," having its full cooperation in powering up is essential.

Finally, the visualization: As you breathe in, focus your awareness on the top of your head and visualize the power streaming in as a beam of light from your over-soul, enhanced and focused by your spirit helpers. Then, as you breathe out, shift your focus to your midsection and visualize the power descending through your head, neck, and chest, coming to rest within your third chakra, which is located behind and slightly above your navel.

Continue this cycle of deep breathing for four to eight breaths, and with each, draw the power in through your head with the in-breath, and then gather it behind your navel as you breathe out. The shift of focus from your head to your navel is what does it. With each completed breath, see the light in your third chakra, your power center, grow brighter. Be alert for any physical sensations in your body indicating power augmentation.

With practice, you can do this exercise anywhere and anytime, whenever there's a need.

≋ ≋ ≋

25
True Magic

ONCE you become power-filled, use your mental soul to create a thoughtform of something that you strongly wish to acquire or experience in your everyday reality. This is the first step to manifesting that something into your life. Remember the fourth rule—when you alter your garden, subtracting or adding something to that place of power—some aspect of you or your life will shift in response.

When you create something in your garden and then pay close attention to it every time you go there, your focused concentration causes energy to flow into the thoughtform. Energy flows where your attention goes, and with repetition, a strong energetic field will take form within and around the thoughtform—a field whose density will increase until it has the power to act as an energetic magnet that may attract the nearest available equivalent experience to you in your outer life.

Remember—the more energy you have, the more you can accomplish. It's in this manner that all true magic works. Knowing this, you can create a shift in your physical, mental, or emotional health, producing a miraculous healing from a supposedly incurable illness. If you want something strongly enough, you'll probably get it—so be careful what you ask for.

Suppose you're suffering from something serious like cancer, Crohn's disease, AIDS, or hepatitis C. You might go into your garden on a daily basis, connect with power, then use whatever visualization you care to create to reverse the illness's effects and diminish its presence in your body.

You might invite a spiritual healing master to come into your garden to work on you—or better yet, a team of specialists. Think of all the renowned compassionate healers across the millennia: Imhotep of Egypt, Aesculapius and Hippocrates of Greece, Avalokiteshvara of India, Kwan Yin of China, Jesus of Nazareth, Galen of Pergamum, Paracelsus during the Renaissance, Florence Nightingale, and Albert Schweitzer or Mother Teresa in our own time.

Needless to say, there are countless numbers of compassionate healing spirits, and they emanate from all cultural traditions. It is through them, and through their connection with us, that we may penetrate to the original cause of our affliction, neutralize its spiritual/energetic complex (which is living within us), and embark on our path of recovery with these healers' full and loving support.

When you're in your garden, you can invite any or all of these great healers to be on your team, whenever there's a need. Their embodiments walked this earth for countless incarnations, so they all know what suffering is. We can connect with them through their oversoul fields.

In our own practice of spirit medicine, it's quite astonishing to note how often the spirit of Jesus of Nazareth will come, offering healing through the power of unconditional love, regardless of whether or not the sufferer is psychologically Christian.

Once in connection with these healing masters, you can ask them to help restore your body to a state of harmony, surrendering to their ministrations and allowing yourself to experience their compassion, as well as their healing power, in your time of need. With practice, this healing energy can also be extended to others, as we shall see shortly.

≋ ≋ ≋

26

A Healing Ritual in the Garden

SELECT a time that's good for you, and while listening to the CD, journey to your garden. When you get there, use your creative imagination to make a healing space. It might be as simple as a circle of stones on an earthen mound beneath an old grandmother tree, or it might be as complex as a room in a magnificent temple in the Greek, Egyptian, or Mayan tradition.

When the place of healing is established in your garden, observe it carefully. Enhance your power by the deep breathing method already outlined in Chapter 24. When you feel that you're power-filled, put out the call for a team of healing masters to come. Invite them to join you in your garden in your time of need—and your need is what empowers your connection with them. The greater your need, the stronger will be their response. And rest assured, if you ask specifically for spirit healers, that's who will come.

Welcome these esteemed healers as they arrive. They could very well be a cluster of indigenous spirits—great medicine women and medicine men all. Acknowledge and honor them, even if you're not sure who they are. Remember, you're the one who put out the call, and they're the ones who have responded to it.

When all are present, invite them to sit around or within the healing space you've created, then explain what you require. Be specific. These are great healers, so there's no need to dissemble or make yourself small. When interacting with these spirits, it's not about worship; it's about relationship. Ask them for support, power, and protection, and make your case.

If you're suffering from a life-threatening illness, you might indicate that you haven't yet fulfilled your life's purpose and that you need their help in prolonging your life so that you can do so. There may also be other compelling reasons for enlisting their assistance. Consider these reasons carefully, and discuss them openly with your visitors.

Then step into your place of healing and invite them to encircle you. Listen to the sound of the drums and the rattles, and watch as these great healers go into a deep meditative trance, enabling them to connect with the universal power of the Source so that they can extend it to you in a healing capacity. Instruct your body soul to accept their healing intentions for you. Ask your inner healer to internalize the energy they extend to you and *use it to erase any distortions in your field, replacing them with light.*

Maybe you'll see these healing masters as the ones beating their drums and shaking their rattles, supporting you with their collective power. Perhaps they'll sing over you and you'll hear their healing songs merging with the drumming and rattling. Perhaps they'll dance around you while drumming and rattling.

Don't be surprised if one of these healing masters steps forward to be of service to you. Perhaps these spirit doctors will do a shamanic extraction for you. Watch as they scan your field with their eyes and their hands, feeling for the illness intrusions and pulling them out. This might also be a team effort with several healers working together, even with a power animal or a plant spirit helper assisting.

See the intrusions that are extracted from your body. How do they appear, and what do your healing masters then do with them? Feel the relief in your body as the intrusions are removed. Watch as your spirit healers bend down and refill the newly vacated spaces in your field with their breath—with their healing breath of power. Feel the sense of warmth as this is done, and know with absolute certainty that a corner has been turned and that you're now fully on the road to recovery.

Continue to listen to the CD, and rest in the beauty of the healers' unlimited compassion for you. Feel their healing intentions flow into you like water filling a bottle. Allow their presence to manifest a deep and abiding sense of safety and tranquility within you.

Know with newfound confidence that your body-mind-spirit complex is in complete harmony in that moment and that your balance is being restored. Using whatever visualization seems right, "see" your illness diminishing as your sense of well-being grows . . . and grows . . . and grows.

When you hear the return beat on the CD, the rapid-fire drumming and rattling, take leave of your spirit friends, asking them to remain on call for repeated healing work in your garden. Then shift the focus of your attention back to your physical body.

Feel the tranquility in your body as you make detailed notes of the journey just completed. Maintain that feeling as long as you can, and remember it throughout your day. Refresh it with another garden ritual when the time seems right.

You're now in relationship with your healing masters, your "astral doctors." Invite them to meet with you in your garden on a regular basis. Often, someone new will show up to be of service to you.[17]

≋ ≋ ≋

27
The Spirit-Medicine Dance

HW: There's an indigenous method for making connection with the spirit of an ancestor who possessed particular skills during life that have been lost across time—knowledge of which we may have urgent need in the present moment. The method that follows was designed to help facilitate such connections in order to recover this lost knowledge.

The technique was known by different names in different cultures, and it was performed in various ways as people adapted it to their needs. The goal, the intention, was always the same, however, and I suspect that it was virtually universal at one time. Since we're focused specifically upon shamanic healing, we could call it *the spirit-medicine dance.*

This exercise is one that we use in our workshops. It allows us to expand our conscious awareness and step outside of time in order to make contact with the spirit of an ancestor who was a great shaman in life, a man or a woman who was an accomplished healer and practitioner of spirit medicine. Most Westerners don't know much about their ancestors beyond their grandparents or great-grandparents, but if we go back far enough, all of us are descended from tribal peoples who had great shamans. Since you're reading this book, it's more than likely that there were shamans among your ancestors, producing imprints in your energetic field and tapping in to a subconscious (body soul) impulse that has nudged you back toward the ancient path of the shaman once again.

The spirit-medicine dance can be done in groups, in a large space indoors, or outside in the beauty of nature, using live drums and rattles. It may also be done at home, alone, in the privacy of your own living space using the CD. Needless to say, this CD can also be used for indoor groups when played on a big sound system.

The goal of the spirit-medicine dance is to step out of time and find connection with an ancestor who was a powerful shaman and healer in life so that we can invite this ancestral spirit to come into relationship with us and join our team of spirit helpers, teachers, and healing masters. The indigenous peoples know that ancestors have a particular concern for their descendants, and rest assured, if you turn your attention in their direction, they will perceive your "call," and one or more may step forward to be of service to you.

If you're at home, create a sacred space with a small altar, and light a candle and some incense perhaps. Turn off your phones and your lights, then utilizing the CD, listen to the drums and the rattles and allow the rhythm to sink into your body. Close your eyes, and allow your body to follow the rhythm . . . until you begin to move. Since the CD track extends for an hour, you have plenty of time. Allow yourself to relax into the rhythm, and let your dance take form.

As you find your way into your dance, bring up the memory of your sacred garden. With your eyes shut, or almost so, go there so that you're dancing in your garden. Create a special place in your garden, a dancing ground, perhaps, where you may dance with your spirits. Perhaps you'll see them, just there at the edges of your vision, drumming and rattling for you.

Continue to find your way into the dance, and as you do, focus your mind, your mental soul, upon finding connection with an ancestral spirit who was a shaman and a great healing master. Hold the intention with fierce concentration as you dance in your garden. Simply maintain your focus, as it is your intentionality that will provide the contact with the one that you're seeking.

Perhaps this will be one of your biological ancestors, a personage from your mother's lineage, or your father's. But there's also another possibility. Perhaps you were a shaman in a past life, even across many past lives. With that thought, the *aka* connection between you and your oversoul may be activated, and the one you're seeking may suddenly appear before you.

This can be startling, to say the least. Try to maintain your focus as you observe the one who has come into your garden. He or she may appear as they were in life, and you may notice details of their clothing, their stature, and facial features. You may feel an immediate sense of connection with them, pervaded by an overwhelming feeling of familiarity.

There may be a strong emotional response to this reunion, for that's exactly what this is—a "family reunion" across the vast reaches of space-time. You may suddenly remember their name, and with that awareness, imagery from the past—soul memories—may flow into you from your visitor through your oversoul. Smile at the one who has come, and offer your respectful greetings, accompanied by your warm-hearted *aloha*. Introduce yourself to them. Tell them who you are and explain why you've called upon them.

If you're not sure who they are or what their name might be, ask them: "Who are you? How is it that are you the one who has come to me? How are (were) we in relationship (in the past)? How can you be of service to me . . . and I to you?" Try to pay close attention, because when you ask a spirit a question, whatever happens next is part of the answer—there may be words, images, or memories from the past. Invite the one who has come to join you on your dancing ground. Feel the joy bubble up within you as the awareness that you're not alone, and never have been, pervades your essence with absolute certainty. Share your joy at this reunion with the one who has come to you. Extend your gratitude and your appreciation.

If you feel like dropping down to continue your journey in a prone or sitting position, do so. The goal of the spirit-medicine dance has been achieved, and you're now in connection with your ancestor. There's a phenomenon that must be mentioned, one that often happens in doing shamanic work—you may unexpectedly experience a spirit move into your field and merge with you. Don't be surprised if this happens with your ancestral shaman. This holy person may do so in order to convey energy and information to you, and he or she may actually *dance you*.

Under such circumstances, it's important not to descend into fear. Remember, you're in relationship with an ally, a spirit who's compassionately concerned for you and who has your very best interests at heart. This spirit has come at your invitation, and as the boundaries between you and the other become blurred, you may acquire that spirit's knowledge and abilities, in the process gaining great insight into the nature of many things.

Although the experience of trance-mediumship (or channeling) is considered to be *paranormal* in the West, it's very much a part of the mainstream in many modern societies in Africa, Latin America, Asia, and Indonesia. Allow the connection to develop within you, exploring its edges and parameters, and when the session comes to a close, express your gratitude once again, and respectfully invite the spirit to detach. Remember, you're the boss in your relationships with spirits in the sacred realms. This is why the shaman is almost universally known as the *master of spirits*.

One other thing needs to be mentioned here. When your ancestor arrives, he or she may come in with a bevy of their own spirits, especially the ones who served them in life. You may become aware of them, just there beyond the edge of your vision, dancing with the two of you. This is a very good sign. Your ancestor may draw upon these spirits to be of service, and you, by association, may acquire a whole new contingency of spiritual allies and helpers.

Let me also note here for those who may be suffering from ongoing depression that it's very difficult to stay depressed when you're moving. If you're feeling low, dance with your spirits in your sacred garden on a daily basis, and this will help lift your depression. Incorporate this spirit-medicine dance into your daily routine—with joy.

≈ ≈ ≈

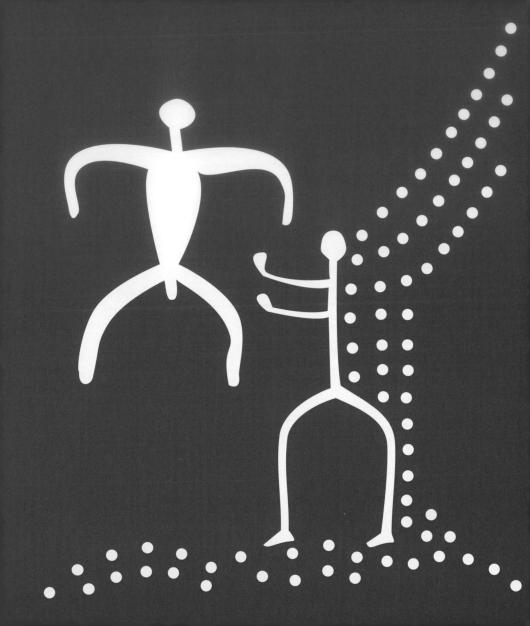

28

A Journey to the Spirit of Illness

HW: Many years ago, a woman in one of my work-shops selected a particular place to be her sacred garden. When she returned from her first journey there, she was puzzled. The place was not as she remembered it. For starters, it had thorny, unfriendly looking vines growing all over everything, choking the trees and blanketing the elements that made the place so charming.

As I listened to her account, a message arrived in my mind, a download from my oversoul, and on impulse, I asked her if she had cancer. Her eyes widened as she confirmed my intuition. She had recently been diagnosed with this disease.

From the shamanic perspective, the unrestrained growth in her garden was symbolic of the out-of-control cell division in her body. I asked her another question, and again, her answer confirmed my suspicion. A series of recent life losses had created a profound sense of disharmony within her. "What shall I do?" she asked me with fear growing in her eyes.

"Well," I responded lightly, "you could sharpen up your metaphysical machete and start chopping the vines out. Or you could do what I do. I was born in New York and lived in an apartment during my early years. Consequently, I'm great with plants in pots, but I'm not skilled at full-fledged landscaping. So when something really big needs my attention, I invite master gardeners into my garden."

She laughed as I suggested that she do the same—invite a team of spirit gardeners to help her chop all the vines out of her garden. She followed my advice in the journeys that followed, yet when the weekend workshop came to a close, she and her gardeners were still chopping—they'd barely made a dent in the still-growing vines.

I suggested that she go to her garden several times each day, as time allowed, and that she continue to work on the vines with help of the spirit gardeners. She did so (in addition to her chemotherapy), and when a letter arrived from her several months later, it contained good news. She and her spirit helpers had finally succeeded in removing all the vines from her garden. Not a sprout or shoot remained. Not surprisingly, when she next visited her oncologist, it was discovered that she was cancer-free.

If you're struggling with a serious illness or chronic affliction, you might take a more active role in your own healing by meeting with the spirit of your illness in your garden and confronting it directly. This could also happen spontaneously as a healing dream.

For instance, I remember a healing dream that I had more than 30 years ago—an extremely vivid one in which I was out in Africa, wading along the edge of a shallow, jungly river, looking for fossils in the eroded riverbank. Suddenly, I found myself face-to-face with a crocodile. It was a real monster, and it was much too close.

After a moment's hesitation, it began to close in. I desperately tried to escape up the steep riverbank, but the sticky brown mud impeded my progress, and the croc was almost upon me. Perhaps the shock of knowing that I couldn't possibly get away triggered what happened next.

While my physical body continued to sleep, I "woke up" in my dream and realized that the whole scenario—the African river, the mud, and the crocodile—was all a dream. With that understanding, I swiveled around, and raising my arm, I pointed at the giant reptile and shouted "Stop!" The croc slid to a halt an arm's length away.

I stared into its yellow eyes and demanded to know why it was pursuing me. A telepathic response came immediately, "I am your tobacco addiction." Stunned, I stared at the creature and noticed for the first time that the brown mud caked all over it looked like the tar I cleaned out of my pipes. Suddenly, I smelled that familiar, rancid tobacco odor emanating from the creature.

Then something unexpected happened. The reptile shifted somehow, transforming itself from pursuer into pal, appearing more like a pet or a harmless circus animal, but it was too late. I had seen it for what it really was. My resolve formed, and I proclaimed with absolute authority, "You're outta here. I no longer need you in my life," and instantly, the croc was gone.[18]

This was the turning point in my battle to give up smoking. From that day forward, I never had another cigarette . . . and I never looked at crocs in quite the same way either. From the perspective of spirit medicine, I confronted the spirit of my addiction in the dream world, did battle with it, and won. Even though it tried to turn itself into an ally, I saw it for what it was and remained steadfast. I haven't smoked tobacco since that dream.

If you're dealing with an addiction or an illness, here's a suggestion for a journey to its spirit. While listening to the CD, go to your garden and practice relaxation. Feel the tranquility of this wonderful place. Allow it to calm you.

When you feel settled, call for your most powerful spirit helpers to come. When they arrive, tell them that you plan to confront the spirit of your illness. Ask them to provide you with power to the max, as well as protection and support. Then, with your spirit helpers' assistance, power up. You can use the breathing method, outlined above, while "seeing" the energy streaming into you as beams of light from your spiritual allies.

When you're power-filled, find a trail at your garden's edge, one that leads off through the foliage, trees, or grasslands down into a lower area that's clearly separate from your personal place of refuge. This will be your battleground. Ask your helpers to accompany you, and then go there.

When you arrive, pick a spot that appeals to you in some way, a place of advantage, perhaps a large stone with a flat summit upon which you can stand high up above the ground. Then, call for the spirit of the illness to come. When it appears, observe it closely: What is it? How does it look? Does it seem threatening? Friendly? Remember, your helping spirits are with you, so there's nothing to fear. You are safe and are just about to reverse the course of your illness.

You may enter into brief conversation, just as I did with the crocodile, but don't be fooled if it shifts to appear charming or amiable. This is not a good guy, not someone you want connected with you. Think about your spirit helpers, and how they've filled you with power, and allow your inner director, your chief, to emerge.

Then bring up your full power and confront the illness spirit. Order it to leave you. See it diminished and beaten down, and banish it from your life forever. If there's any resistance, ask your spirit helpers to do battle for you, and they will. Don't be surprised if someone unexpected shows up to assist. If your illness spirit has chosen to manifest itself to you as a crocodile or a dragon, the new ally could be St. George, or even Archangel Michael with his sword of light.

This doesn't mean that crocodiles or dragons are evil, by the way. It's simply a form that your illness has chosen to take in confronting you. The spirit of your sickness could appear as anything, even as a sacred being, a saint, a prophet, or an angel. Your task lies in seeing through its shape-changing trickery—in seeing it for what it really is, and remaining firm in your resolve.

When the sickness spirit has vanished, return up the trail to your garden. Does anything appear different? Ask your defenders to join you, and have a talk with them. Express your gratitude and ask them to remain on guard until all vestiges of the illness have left your body.

Since your body soul is the self-aspect through which you journey into your garden, it has witnessed all that transpired. Ask if there's anything it needs or wants. You may get a surprise. It could be an espresso at your favorite café, a cuddle with your lover, a swim at your favorite beach, or even a hot fudge sundae.

Use your mental soul to create a thoughtform of whatever it is your body soul needs and offer it. Then, when your body soul is sparkling happily, instruct it to start restoring your energetic matrix to its former undistorted state. As the blueprint is repaired, your inner healer will go to work once again with a clear pattern to work from.

In this way, you can infuse your inner healer with an enhanced sense of purpose, as well as power and support from your spirits. Remember, your body soul does not distinguish between reality and illusion, but takes everything literally. So from the body's perspective, the vision is real, as well as the thoughtform of the gift you created for it.

Knowing this, you might adopt a healing meditation, repeated at regular intervals, to reinforce your command—to heal the body.

≋ ≋ ≋

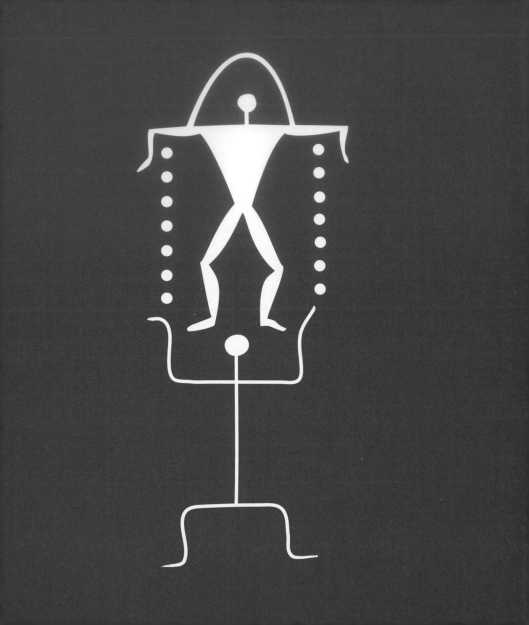

29

A Healing Meditation

IF you have a serious health issue, it would be wise to do a healing meditation for 30 minutes or more, at least once or twice each day.

Meditation is sustained, focused concentration. Your egoic mental soul derives its power from the control it exerts on your attention. When your attention is focused upon something, that's where the power goes. Focused attention becomes intent, and your body soul, picking up on this, implements the intent. The ability to hold your focus will improve with practice.

The goal of the meditation that follows is to connect with your oversoul and ask it to channel power to you in a healing capacity. In doing so, you'll be asking your immortal self to defend the mortal. Simply knowing that this is going on will enhance the functioning of your immune system dramatically.

The CD track runs for an hour, so you have plenty of time. While listening to it, go to your garden and step into your special healing place. Practice relaxation, and allow the tranquility of your garden to calm you.

Take a few moments and forgive those in your life for all the real and imagined wrongs that you perceive. Forgive yourself for the disharmony you've caused in others as well as within yourself. Forgiveness is healing.

Then ask for your healing masters and spirit helpers to come. Greet them warmly, and feel your confidence grow in response to their presence. Refocus your awareness on your body, and visualize your illness. See how it appears to you, as well as where it's located in your body. What color is it? Also look for any negative thoughtforms or fears about your illness. They, as well as your illness, may appear as dark gray or even black shapes.

Focus on your breathing, then turn to your spirit helpers and ask one of them to come forward with the cosmic vacuum cleaner. See this spirit gently running the nozzle through your field from your feet to your head. As you breathe out with each exhalation, release your illness intrusions along with your fears. Release, as well, the pain of your disease, and see the dark knots and granules being sucked up by the vacuum.

When your field is clear of any darknesses and your body soul is free of any doubts or fears, express your appreciation to the one who's served you. Then focus your awareness upwards, and reach for connection with your oversoul, your utterly trustworthy, immortal spirit—the one who hovers over you.

You might suddenly see it as a beautiful glowing orb of light just there, right above you. Greet it with your love. Remember, this is your immortal essence—your god-self. This is "you-there"—the one who loves you, and who will always love you, the one who listens to your prayers.

Redouble your concentration and ask your oversoul to send down its *hā*—its healing breath of power. Watch as the brilliant orb directs a luminous beam into you, sweeping your body with waves of blue light. You may feel a prickly rush of sensation, like the effervescence that appears in your throat in response to a gulp of soda or a glass of champagne.

Perceive those bubbles as your white blood cells awakening and responding to the infusion of power you're receiving. Feel them percolating throughout your entire body, attacking any remaining gray wisps, granules, or fragments, and replace them with blue light. Hold your focus for as long as you wish, and enjoy the sensation.

When you feel ready, ask your oversoul to sweep your being with waves of green light to restore all those cells, tissues, or organs damaged by your illness. Allow the configurations of this healing green light to infuse your weakened body with courage, filling your soul cluster with confidence that your illness is being overcome and your body healed.

Conclude the exercise by asking the beautiful orb hovering above you to descend. Ask it to come close to you, then ask its permission to get inside it. This request is always granted. Feel it surrounding you like a shield of protection. Feel the tranquility flowing within you, and know with absolute certainty that you're within the field of your immortal self—that you're in a state of grace. Feel the joy of reunion, and know for sure that you're loved.

Then turn your thoughts toward someone in this life whom you love deeply. Feel your love for that person flowing around and through you. Feel the deep peace of *aloha* within your heart, and then softly repeat these words: "Heal, heal, heal, heal . . ." for as long as you wish.[19]

When you emerge from your meditation, express your gratitude and appreciation to your oversoul. Maintain that feeling of love as long as you can, then let it gently go, knowing that you can reconnect with it again at a moment's notice.

As you repeat this meditation again and again and again, you'll notice that the bubbles in your field will sparkle ever more brightly, and that the initial dimness of your field will glow ever more luminous in response.

≋ ≋ ≋

30
Spirit Medicine
in Groups

HW: In two of my previous books, *Medicinemaker* and *Visionseeker,* I wrote about spiritual healing rituals in which I've been personally involved. I must reiterate once more how impressed I've been by the transformative power these ceremonies obviously convey upon the recipient, many with serious illnesses such as cancer, Crohn's disease, lupus erythematosus, chronic obstructive pulmonary disease, urinary tract dysfunction, prostatitis, multiple sclerosis, chronic pain, leukemia, AIDS, and ventricular tachycardia, as well as less serious problems such as tennis elbow and tendonitis.

There are people accomplished in spirit medicine in virtually every community. It's just a matter of finding them (see Endnote 21). One way to do so is to involve yourself in a drumming circle or a shamanic workshop in or near your home base so that you can make connection with others in your community involved in this work.

In order to provide some guidance to those new to this healing methodology, allow me to describe how Jill and I conduct spirit-medicine ceremonies at our workshops. The basic model that follows provides an outline that's not dependent upon any particular belief system or cultural tradition, and hence it can be considered as "core."

At the close of our workshops, virtually all the participants are in connection with their spirit helpers, spirit teachers, and hopefully with one or more healing masters, so the battery is fully charged, so to speak. This is always a prime opportunity to engage in spirit-medicine work, so we usually ask if there's anyone in the circle who's suffering from a chronic physical problem or life-threatening condition.

Usually someone in need comes forward and requests healing. This request is important, as it establishes their intention, as well as their willingness to participate, which is the first necessary step in their own healing.

As the ritual begins to take form, the workshop participants create a circle around the room's periphery, in the center of which the sufferer lies down on a blanket or sits in a chair. A man and a woman (usually the teachers/facilitators) then kneel or sit on each side of the client, forming an inner center of focus. There's a harmony that comes into being when a man and a woman work together, as this creates a merging of the male and the female, the masculine and the feminine. In this state of balance, healing happens more readily.

To one side of the sufferer, there's usually a small altar on the floor (or low table) with a candle burning in its center, accompanied by incense and various power objects. In addition to serving as a sacred center, the altar also has a most important function.

The indigenous peoples know that sometimes it's necessary to create a doorway between the two halves of the world, between the inner and the outer, between the timeless people (the spirits) and the people of time (ourselves). The altar may serve as this doorway. As the ritual deepens and the spirits are summoned, the aperture within the altar opens so that the holy beings can pass through it into our world to be of service to us. The spirits have been doing this for a very long time. This is a known experience for them.

At the ceremony's inception, prayers are offered, with each person addressing their spirit helpers, teachers, and healing masters, establishing their intention for healing, and requesting assistance in the medicine work to follow.

In the outer circle, each individual commences drumming or rattling, establishing a strong, steady rhythm to assist in the expansion of consciousness of the entire group. As each enters into the trance state, we put out a call to our spirits—to our helpers, teachers, and healing masters—and we ask them to come into the room, to stand behind us and connect with us, so that they can begin to convey the great power into us.

Often, if not always, we perceive physical sensations associated with this augmentation of our personal power. As we become power-filled, we intentionally raise the energy to the level of our heart because this is where connection with the energy of compassion takes place. This is where we make contact with the transpersonal force that the *kahunas* call *aloha*.

Then, with our spirits still in connection with us and the energy of compassion surging through us, we simply fasten our attention on the one suffering in the center of the circle. Energy flows where your attention goes, so all you have to do is hold your focus. The rest will take care of itself. This means that you don't have to do anything to anyone, because in the practice of spirit medicine, you're not doing it! The spirits are working with and through you, and they're the ones who are actually carrying out the healing work. Even if you may not be able to see them, you may sense their benevolent presence and feel their attention resting upon you.

This brings up something truly wonderful. Healing is about receiving. It's not about you doing anything to the sufferer. When you put out the call, announcing that you're willing to be of service to another person in a healing capacity, the compassionate spirits regard this very highly, and they'll come. The healing then happens without you or anyone else having to get personally involved.

This is spirit medicine at its absolute best.

The man and woman working with the sufferer in the circle's center may enhance the ritual by connecting with their spirits to intentionally augment that person's power. They may also do a diagnosis with the aid of their spiritual helpers, followed by extraction of the illness intrusions. Throughout, they're supported and assisted by their spirits, by the drumming and rattling, and by the power that's being accessed and channeled by those in the outer circle.

In this way, each person in the circle is just as important as all the others, forming a healing community that's working together as a unit, focused upon alleviating the pain and suffering of the one at the center.

It should be noted in passing that soul retrieval is often best done in a separate session, with the client working one-on-one with a practitioner accomplished in this healing modality. Soul retrieval unfolds in stages. It is complex, presenting the opportunity for the client to create "the call" for their healing, as well as the practitioner's journeywork. Such sessions usually extend for several hours, with follow-up work to be done by the client afterward.

≈ ≈ ≈

31
Healing Long Distance

HW: At the ritual's end, we often do long-distance work for those in need of healing who couldn't be present at the workshop. This may also be done when you're alone, in which case the garden may be a good place from which to connect with your spirits, as well as with the person in need.

It's important to remember that correct protocol requires that the person who's suffering ask for your help. It's not appropriate to enforce healing upon the unwilling, nor is it correct to volunteer or push your services upon someone who's ill, as this may produce confusion, conflict, or even resentment within them or their family—and this is the last thing you want to create under the circumstances.

Their request for help is essential because (1) it represents their commitment toward working *with* you; (2) it activates the *aka* cord, as well as the heart connection, that links the two of you together; and (3) accepting what spirit medicine has to offer them is the *necessary* first step toward their healing.

Without commitment, acceptance, and investment in their own well-being, not much may happen. As has been indicated, people heal themselves . . . and sometimes, being in connection with a powerful healer in whom they have confidence increases their body soul's ability to go to work and do what it's programmed to do with an enhanced sense of purpose.

Sometimes there's an emergency, however, in which someone is in crisis, in the hospital, or even in surgery, and they can't ask for help. If you have a strong heart connection with such a person, and if you know *with absolute certainty* that they would be mad with joy if you did healing work on their behalf, you can regard this as acceptance.

In doing long-distance work, several approaches are possible. Perhaps the simplest and most powerful way is to begin by going to your garden and summoning your spirit helpers while listening to the CD. When they arrive, go to your healing place, inviting them to join you there, and then inform them about the one in need. (If you're part of a group involved in doing a healing ritual, you're already in the healing space and are in touch with the spirits who are serving you.)

Tell the spirits that you require their help in doing a healing for your friend or family member. Take your time in doing so because you're building your case and establishing intention, both of which are critical to the success of what you're about to do. As you focus your thoughts upon the one who's suffering, you're also activating your *aka* connection with them.

Use your mental soul to create your intention—to send power in a healing capacity to your friend in need, and then ask your spirit helpers to connect with you and channel energy into you big time, filling you with power. Remember, these spirits are the extension cords between you and the power of the universe, and you, like the indigenous shaman, are using your own body as the link between your spirits and your friend.

When you feel yourself to be power-filled, bring up your friend or family member in your mind's eye. When you can see them clearly, raise the power in your body to the level of your heart, and get in touch with the love you feel for the one in need. That feeling is your connecting link with them. It also energizes your *aka* cord of connection to them.

Then . . . simply whisper or say their name out loud. At that instant, the power you've gathered will receive that infusion immediately, accompanied by your love for that person. This is what's called *nonlocal* work, and their body soul (as perceiver/receiver) will take it in and go to work (as the inner healer) from a place of enhanced empowerment.

Remember—there's no power in the universe as strong as the power of love—what the *kahunas* call *aloha*.

The indigenous peoples also know a great secret. Every time you send an arrow of power in a healing capacity to someone else, that arrow has two opposite points, and the energy flows in both directions. This means that every time you offer healing to someone else, you receive healing yourself.

This is why medicinemakers often live to be very old.

≋ ≋ ≋

32

Ancestral Lineage Healing

HW: The energy body is a composite field derived from three sources—the energy of the mother, that of the father, and the energetic infusion from our personal oversoul. These three fields are links of connection, in turn, with our ancestral past, and since energy never dies, we can't disconnect from those who've given life to us.

These fields record imprints of everything that happened within the lives of our ancestors. Lifetimes dominated by positive focus and good intentions produce lineages oriented toward positive action, personal growth, and accomplishment. In the same manner, negative goals or unsavory actions across many generations may result in imprints of abuse, illness, and misfortune. In the Eastern traditions, the creation of such patterns is called *karma*.

Those ancestors who have crossed over most recently are the ones with whom we have the closest links, both biologically and spiritually. If a serious illness or severe life trauma was endured by one or more of these individuals, it's recorded within their energy system. And since they're only removed from us by a generation or two, those conditions may affect us, producing distortions in our own fields that can manifest as illness. Here's an example.

When I was in my early 50s, I developed a sore throat that never seemed to get better. I had been a heavy tobacco smoker earlier in life, so I went to an ear, nose, and throat specialist. Nothing abnormal was detected, there was nothing to biopsy, so I was sent home with allergy pills.

Six months later, my sore throat was still very much alive. Another medical examination revealed nothing. More allergy pills. A year later, the same. So I turned my attention toward my spirit teachers for answers to this quandary, and their response produced an unexpected insight.

When my mother's father was in his early 50s, he developed throat cancer, and in the surgical procedure that followed, his larynx and part of his throat were removed. He survived his cancer, although he spoke in a whisper for the rest of his life, one that extended well into his 80s. Yet the throat cancer and the subsequent surgery had caused the distortion in his field, creating an energetic wound that was still present even after the death of his physical body.

Many indigenous groups, including the Taoists in northern China and Korea, know that the energy body can maintain its integration as a personal pattern long after death. They say that it takes approximately four generations, or up to a hundred years, for an ancestor's energy to completely detach from this world. It's also known that ancestors often feel a particular concern for their descendants, and they may remain in connection with them, serving as guides, protectors, and teachers.

I thought about this at some length. Could it be that the discordance in my grandfather's field was affecting me adversely, producing my chronic sore throat? My grandfather and I had loved each other dearly in life, so I understood quite clearly that this wasn't being done deliberately. Perhaps it simply couldn't be avoided because of the closeness of the connection.

This brought up a series of intriguing questions. Did my grandfather need to be healed before he could ascend back into the Upper Worlds and rejoin his oversoul source? Was this why the symptoms had appeared in my throat? And could I, using the techniques of spirit medicine, heal my grandfather?

The answers to such questions remain elusive, yet there was also a sense of urgency. If I couldn't heal my grandfather, dead for 40 years, would I manifest cancer in my own throat? I was the same age that my grandfather had been when he developed the cancer—an age when his immune system's ability to protect him was beginning to decline.

I decided to attempt a healing for my grandfather, and I did what all practitioners of spirit medicine do under such circumstances. I turned toward my spirit helpers for advice and guidance. My meeting with them revealed that one possibility was to invite my grandfather's spirit into my sacred garden and do the healing there with the assistance of my healing masters. Then, an interesting idea presented itself: Why not try to find my grandfather in *his* sacred garden?

Many indigenous groups understand that when we die, we go into a dream from which we don't wake up. These postmortem states are dreamed by the dying, and they appear to be archetypically determined. That means that they tend to take forms derived from the worldview of the dreamer.

These dreams are "in between" states located in the Middle World of Level Three. They're situated between the life just lived and the return of our energetic matrix to our oversoul field in the Upper Worlds. As has been mentioned, the Tibetans call these the *Bardo worlds*. Christians refer to them as *purgatory*.

Understanding this, I went into journey-mode, expanding my consciousness, and then I intentionally connected with my grandfather's spirit through that part of my own energetic matrix that's derived from his. Upon doing so, I discovered that when he died, my grandfather had entered into the dreaming of the garden that had surrounded the house he'd lived in, and that's exactly where I found him, sitting on a bench, surrounded by foliage—a place that he'd been very fond of in life.

Knowing that my grandfather had last seen me when I was 11 years old, I remembered myself at that age, essentially re-creating myself as the boy that I knew my grandfather would recognize. I then approached the elder gentleman seated on his bench in the dream world, and our reunion was a warm one.

Remember, my grandfather was outside the time-space continuum, and so it meant nothing that 40 years had passed on the physical plane of Level One.

As we chatted about this and that, much as we'd done in life, I kept glancing at his throat. How was I to do a spirit-medicine healing for this patrician gentleman who had owned the beautiful house called Seven Doors on the island of Nantucket?

I appealed to my spirits, and their response was immediate. On impulse, I got up and stepped behind the bench, whereupon my grandfather looked the other way and pretended not to see me. This had been a game we'd played when I was a small child, a game in which I would sneak up behind my grandfather through the bushes and then suddenly jump up to place my hands over his eyes from behind. *Guess who?*

On this occasion, I looked down at the pine needles carpeting the ground behind the bench and made my intention. Instantly, from between the pine needles, the head of a garter snake appeared, and then another—the same snakes I'd caught and kept in a coffee can as pets when I was a child. They were still there, in the dreaming of my grandfather's garden.

Without thinking, I put my hands down on the ground, and the striped snakes promptly wrapped their long bodies around my forearms. Then I stood and gently placed my hands over my grandfather's eyes. Instantly, the old man became immobile and began to ask: "Is it Clark Gable? Nooo . . . Errol Flynn? Noooo . . . David Niven? Noooo . . . Lionel Barrymore? Nooo . . ." and so on down the list.

Meanwhile, the snakes dropped their heads down to the level of his neck and began to flick their double-tongues over the wound in his throat. I had no idea what they were doing. Perhaps it was some form of snake medicine. I concentrated upon healing for my grandfather and held fiercely to my focus. The snakes continued flicking away with their tongues until my grandfather guessed correctly, whereupon the old gentleman leaned back to be embraced by his grandson.

For long moments, I simply held my grandfather in my arms, our hearts brimming with the great affection we had for each other. Then I released him and dropped my arms. The snakes took this as a cue and dropped down, gliding off into the brush, unseen by the old man. As the drumming came to an end, I took my leave, promising to return on the morrow.

This was the first "ancestral healing" I did for my grandfather, but on checking my own throat afterward, not much seemed to have changed. *Maybe there's a cumulative effect,* I thought. So I made follow-up journeys to my grandfather during my workshops on the weekends that followed.

Several weeks later, I noted with interest that my sore throat had improved, and over the next several months, it disappeared completely. A subsequent journey to my grandfather's garden revealed that the old man was gone. His wound had been healed . . . and he had ascended.

This is just one example illustrating how it may be possible to work with our spirit helpers—and by association, with subtle energies—repairing distortions that accumulate within families across time. In the process, the collective matrices of ancestral lineages may be freed of pain and suffering, and the wounds passed generationally from parent to child, even from oversoul to descendant self, may be healed.

It has already been noted that when we enter the timeless dimensions of the dream and do a spirit-medicine healing for someone else, we receive healing for ourselves, as well as for the macrocosm mirrored inside us, with all its fears and struggles, hopes and dreams.

This means that when we engage in healing work of any kind, we do a healing for the world.

≋ ≋ ≋

33

The Medicinemaker

MANY who are good at facilitating the art of healing have walked the path of illness themselves. This is
why the shaman, the master practitioner of spirit medicine, is often known as "the wounded healer."

True medicinework begins with dealing with our own
issues. How we choose to respond to our life challenges
results in our experiencing many levels of initiation, both
the positive as well as the negative. Deepened self-realization results, and it is then that the process of self-healing

truly begins. That's why this book begins with a consideration of self-nature and concludes with exercises devoted toward self-healing.

Once we've restored ourselves with the full and loving support of our spirit helpers, we can begin to extend our knowledge and abilities outward into the fabric of the community, with these wise beings serving as our advisors and teachers. Through direct experience, we learn that healing is primarily an act of spirit, as Papa Henry gently advised, and not the result of personal will plus pharmaceuticals, although they, too, play their parts.

It should be mentioned that as we become spirit-medicine practitioners ourselves, we should only work up to our personal level of experience and training. If you've heard or read about soul retrieval, for example, it would be wise to study with an accomplished teacher of this healing modality before attempting to perform it yourself.

Having brought this up, we should observe that many often ask us if soul retrieval can be done for oneself. The answer is "That depends . . ." People do, on occasion, experience spontaneous returns, and sometimes they can indeed call back parts of their soul cluster. But we've also observed that soul retrieval is specialty work, and not all shamans are good at it. It's complex, and those who can do it, and do it well, are in a league of their own as healers. This is why those in need of soul retrieval would be well advised to seek connection with an accomplished practitioner of this work.[20]

The same holds true for other specialized areas such as shamanic extraction, as well as entity depossession. It's best to learn how to work with these healing modalities by studying with someone who knows what they're doing.[21]

The hands-on experiential approach in a structured workshop setting may provide us with tools and techniques that are necessary for the success of our endeavors as healers. Accordingly, opportunities to work with accomplished teachers and to participate in healing rituals should be chosen whenever possible. Through connection and cooperation with others with similar orientations and training, our experience is broadened, our abilities sharpen to become more refined, and our knowledge deepens to become wisdom.

The bottom line is that there's always more power in a group. When a half dozen or more are connected to their spirit helpers, each can then serve as a bridge, conveying the power in a healing capacity to the sufferer. The results can be immediate and dramatic . . . and they may also be subtle and cumulative.

As we've already mentioned, the key is no doubt . . .

≋ ≋ ≋

"Hale Makua, Keeper of the Past"

34
The Kahuna

HW: Since this book begins with an account of our relationship with a Hawaiian *kahuna* healer, it seems appropriate for us to close with a brief story involving one other.

Many years ago, Jill and I were drawn into connection with Hale Makua, a seventh-generation descendant, through his mother's lineage, of King Kamehameha and his third wife, Kahaku Ha'a Koi Wahine Pio. Through his father, he was a seventh-generation descendant of High Chief Keoua Kuahu'ula, the son of High Chief Kalaniopu'u, making his genealogy exceptional, to say the least.[22]

On the last day of 1996, Makua, as he was generally known, took us to the vast caldera of Kilauea in what is today known as Hawai'i Volcanoes National Park on the southeastern side of the Big Island. As we walked together along a ridge called Uwe Kahuna, 500 feet above the frozen lake of stone, he paused and began to chant in Hawaiian. He called in the spirits of his ancestors to witness our meeting, extending an invitation as well to the volcano spirit Pele whose traditional place of residence, Halema'uma'u, was directly below us. It was there that our friendship took root and began to grow.

Toward the end of that long day, Makua suddenly and unexpectedly gave us a gift—a simple Hawaiian bowl fashioned of *kamani* wood. "This is your bowl of light," he intoned with dignity. "This light is the essence that you brought into this life, a gift from your *aumakua,* which divided itself." He looked thoughtful as he turned the bowl this way and that. "As we pass through life, things happen. Sometimes we take things that don't belong to us; sometimes we injure others through our words, our thoughts, or our actions; sometimes we achieve success at the expense of the failure of others. Whenever such things happen, we step into the negative polarity, and some of our light goes out."

He smiled wistfully as he finished his thought: "Each time we do this, it is like we put a stone into our bowl." He paused for a long time. "Eventually our bowl fills up with stones, and no light is forthcoming anymore."

The *kahuna* elder turned to us in the twilight and said, "Hopefully, we come to realize what we are doing before it fills completely. Do you know what you do then?" He abruptly burst into laughter, his full gray beard and long white hair quivering with mirth around his dark face. He flipped the bowl over deftly and shook it. "You dump it out!" More laughter, shared by us all. Then his gaze turned serious once again.

"When we come to realize what we have been doing, we begin to live our lives differently. And it is then, precisely then, that we start to walk our path as spiritual warriors."

The elder looked us over slowly. "As spiritual warriors, our path is narrow, and it is constrained by three *kapus,* three sacred directives. Since you have reached that place of knowing, I can offer these three *kapus* to you:

> *Love all that you see, with humility . . .*
> *Live all that you feel, with reverence . . .*
> *Know all that you possess, with discipline.*

In those moments, surrounded by flowering *ohia* trees, scrubby *ohelo* bushes, and ferns growing directly out of the volcanic stone in the dying light, I was aware that something quite rare had just occurred. I glanced at Jill. There were tears gathering in her eyes.

Makua just smiled, and a silence descended as we digested his words. "When we come from a place of humility," he continued gently, "we connect with the energy of compassion, allowing us to experience the power of *aloha.* When we accept this *aloha* and live it, we are drawn inexorably toward reverence, an active respect for everyone and everything that we encounter in life. Through knowing what we possess . . . and this includes all that possesses us," more laughter, "we find our discipline. And in order to discover *who* we are, as well as *where* we are, self-discipline is essential, because without it, we cannot progress."

Makua's words triggered a memory of something I'd heard an old indigenous shaman say many years ago:

> *"To be a medicinemaker, one must have well-formed ethics, and one must also possess a generous heart. People can acquire power in life, but if they have poorly formed ethics or underdeveloped hearts, they can't be medicinemakers."*

Makua's spirit passed into the care of his ancestors on March 27, 2004. He enriched the lives of all who knew him with his wisdom and compassion, his humility and laughter, his gallantry and grace. He brought us great joy.

In the practice of spirit medicine, we experience qualities such as humility and reverence, compassion and forgiveness . . . and every moment becomes an opportunity for grace. To enter into this work reflects our honor. To be of service in these ways redeems the world.

So please accept these words and thoughts that come from our hearts to yours . . . with our blessings, and our warmest *aloha*.

≈ ≈ ≈

Endnotes

1. The Hawaiian word *kahuna* has implications that have to do with mastery. A shaman or master of spirits would be a *kahuna kupua;* a ceremonialist or priest would be called a *kahuna pule,* or master of prayer. Papa Henry was a master herbalist healer, or *kahuna la'au lapa'au.*

2. Papa Henry Allen Auwae made transition in his 94th year on New Year's Eve 2000. Those interested may read the following interview: "Papa Henry Auwae: Po'okela La'au Lapa'au, Master of Hawaiian Medicine," in the journal *Alternative Therapies:* vol. 6, no. 1, January 2000, pp. 82–88.

3. See Ronald Goodman, *Lakota Star Knowledge: Studies in Lakota Stellar Theology,* 2nd Ed. (Rosebud, South Dakota: Sinte Gleska University Press, 1992). See also Richard W. Voss, Wo'lakol Kiciyapi: Traditional Philosophies of Helping and Healing among the Lakotas. *Journal of Multicultural Social Work* 7: 73–93, 1999.

4. I (**HW**) first stumbled across the Inuit perception of the three souls through visionary experiences recorded in my book *Spiritwalker* (New York: Bantam Books, 1995).

5. For example, see Max Freedom Long's *The Secret Science Behind Miracles* (Marina del Ray, CA: DeVorss, 1948). More information about the Hawaiian perspective on the three souls may be found in my (**HW's**) Spiritwalker trilogy—*Spiritwalker, Medicinemaker,* and *Visionseeker.* An important review of David Kaonohiokala Bray's teachings, as well as Max Freedom Long's perspectives on the three souls, can be found in Laura Kealoha Yardley's *The Heart of Huna* (Honolulu, HI: Advanced Neurodynamics, Inc., 1982). See also Charlotte Berney's *Fundamentals of Hawaiian Mysticism* (Freedom, CA: The Crossing Press, 2000); Samuel Manaiakalani Kamakau's *Ka Po'e Kahiko: The People of Old* (Honolulu, HI: Bishop Museum Press, 1991); Leinani Melville's *Children of the Rainbow: The Religion, Legends, and Gods of Pre-Christian Hawai'i* (Wheaton, Il: Theosophical Publishing House, 1969); Martha Beckwith's *Hawaiian Mythology* (Honolulu, HI: The University of Hawai'i Press, 1970); and Serge King's *Kahuna Healing* (Wheaton, Il: Theosophical Publishing House, 1983). We are indebted to all these authors, from whom

we've liberally borrowed concepts, precepts, and ideas, as well as ways of organizing this extraordinary information.

6. A more expanded version of this view of reality can be found in my (**HW's**) book *Visionseeker,* Chapter 10. Gratitude is also expressed to Serge King for his clarity and knowledge.

7. A series of excavations at Blombos Cave in South Africa, reported in *Science,* January 2002, have revealed several elongated pieces of red ochre into which web- or gridlike designs have been inscribed. These are (at this time) the earliest examples of symbolic expression. They have been accurately dated to 77,000 years before the present.

8. See, for example, Eligio Gallegos, *The Personal Totem Pole: Animal Imagery, the Chakras, and Psychotherapy* (Santa Fe, NM: Moon Bear Press, 1987), as well as Stanislav Grof's *The Adventure of Self-Discovery* (Albany, NY: SUNY Press, 1988).

9. In Chapter 16 of my (**HW's**) book *Visionseeker,* I have tried to describe my own direct experience with the Source. Whether I succeeded in my attempt remains to be seen . . . but I had to try.

10. My (**HW's**) book *The Journey to the Sacred Garden* discusses the ground for shamanic journeywork in more detail. See also John Mack's *Passport to the Cosmos: Human Transformation and Alien Encounters* (New York: Crown Books, 1999) for a fascinating comparison of shamanism and the UFO experience.

11. I (**HW**) have discussed this at some length with the anthropologist Michael Harner, Ph.D., who believes that about 90 percent of us can "shamanize" to some extent, with about 50 percent of us being real naturals at it. See his book *The Way of the Shaman: A Guide to Power and Healing* (San Francisco: Harper SanFrancisco, 1990). See also Jeremy Narby's *The Cosmic Serpent: DNA and the Origins of Knowledge* (New York: Putnam, 1998).

12. I (**HW**) acknowledge here my debt to Michael Harner. Without his wise guidance and accomplished teachings, the shamanic skills and abilities of thousands of people, including myself, might have remained undeveloped and their program misdiagnosed (i.e., pathologized). His Foundation for Shamanic Studies Website can be accessed at **www.shamanism.org**.

13. See Jeanne Achterberg's "The Shaman: Master Healer in the Imaginary Realm," in Shirley Nicholson (ed.), *Shamanism: An Expanded View of Reality* (Wheaton, IL: Theosophical Publishing House, 1987).

14. See J. Raloff, "Baby's AIDS Virus Infection Vanishes," in *Science News,* 147: p. 196, 1995. We are indebted to Gregg Braden for bringing this study to our attention. It is also cited in Braden's book *Walking Between the Worlds: The Science of Compassion* (Bellevue, WA: Radio Bookstore Press, 1997).

15. See Laura Yardley's *The Heart of Huna,* and also David K. Bray and Douglas Low, *The Kahuna Religion of Hawai'i* (Vista, CA: Borderland Sciences Research Foundation, 1980).

16. See *The Journey to the Sacred Garden,* Chapters 24–27.

17. See Chapter 17 in *Visionseeker* for a dramatic example.

18. A similar experience is recorded in a paper published by Jeremy Taylor called "The Healing Spirit of Lucid Dreaming," in *Shaman's Drum,* Spring 1992, 55–62.

19. See Michael Newton's *Destiny of Souls* (St. Paul, MN: Llewellyn, 2002) for a similar healing meditation.

20. Those interested might begin with Sandra Ingerman's *Soul Retrieval: Mending the Fragmented Self* (San Francisco: Harper SanFrancisco, 1991).

21. Michael Harner's Foundation for Shamanic Studies is an important resource (**www.shamanism.org**) for training workshops, as well as for referrals to shamanic practitioners.

22. Hale Makua's name, as well as the names of his ancestors, are included in this book with his permission. An account of our initial contact with him is recorded in *Visionseeker,* Chapter 15.

≈ ≈ ≈

Shamanic Training Workshops

PERIODICALLY, shamanic healers feel the need to withdraw in order to renew their spiritual contacts and purify themselves so that their energy can continue to flow properly. In the Western world, this can be done by working with other accomplished practitioners and their students in shamanic workshops and training programs.

≈

Interest in shamanic workshops and seminars with Hank Wesselman and Jill Kuykendall can be directed to:

SharedWisdom
P.O. Box 2059
Granite Bay, CA 95746
Website: **www.sharedwisdom.com**

916-553-2951 (voicemail)
916-797-4914 (fax)
E-mail: hank@sharedwisdom.com
E-mail: jill@sharedwisdom.com

About the Authors

HANK Wesselman, Ph.D., holds advanced degrees in anthropology and zoology from the University of California at Berkeley and the University of Colorado at Boulder. He served in the U.S. Peace Corps in the 1960s, living among people of the Yoruba Tribe in Western Nigeria, where he first became interested in indigenous spiritual traditions.

Since 1971, he's conducted research with an international group of scientists, exploring eastern Africa's Great Rift Valley in search of answers to the mystery of human origins—scientific investigation that has allowed him to spend much of his life living and working with traditional peoples, rarely, if ever, visited by outsiders.

Hank has taught for the University of California, San Diego; the University of Hawai'i at Hilo's West Hawai'i Campus; California State University at Sacramento; American River College; and Sierra College; as well as for Kiriji Memorial College and Adeola Odutola College in western Nigeria.

His books include *The Journey to The Sacred Garden: A Guide to Traveling in the Spiritual Realms,* as well as his autobiographical trilogy: *Spiritwalker, Medicinemaker,* and *Visionseeker.*

≋

JILL **Kuykendall, RPT,** is a transpersonal medical practitioner trained in physical therapy at the medical school of the University of California, San Francisco. She also holds a degree in psychology from the University of California at Berkeley. Jill has worked in acute-care rehabilitation and home health within the standard medical paradigm for most of the past 25 years and is currently in private practice at the Center for Optimum Health in Roseville, California, specializing in soul retrieval.

≋

Hank and Jill offer seminars and shamanic training workshops at internationally recognized centers such as the Esalen Institute in California, the Omega Institute near New York, and the New Millennium Institute in Hawai'i. Their schedule and workshop descriptions can be accessed on their Website: **www.sharedwisdom.com.**

Acknowledgments

FIRST and foremost, we offer our gratitude and our deep appreciation to the wonderful children we created together, Erica and Anna Wesselman, who opened our hearts and from whom we've learned so much.

Others who have provided wise guidance and compassionate support over the years include: Kahu Nelita Anderson, Papa Henry Auwae, Hedy and Mario Baldassarrini, Daniel Bianchetta, Linda Blackman, Gregg Braden, Nancy Brown and Bo Clark, David Corbin and Nan Moss, Bo Galieto, Sandra and Michael Harner, Barbara Marx Hubbard, Robin Haines and Cody Johnson, Kahu Hale Kealohalani Makua and Nina Shelofsky, Eva and Mason Ma'ikui, Takeshi Misaki and Noriko Nagato, Joanne and Ernest Reyes, Sr., Kahu Morrnah Simeona, Venice Sullivan, Lili Townsend, Renee VonFeldt, Cynee and Bill Wenner, Susan Whitaker, Jeannie Wiese, and Sandra Wright.

A special thank you to our colleagues and staff at The Center for Optimum Health, to the members of the Tuesday–Thursday Drumming Circle, and to the many wonderful workshop participants and clientele who have shared their wisdom and their lives with us. Jennifer Ann and Lodi Bob Moore, Kimball Parent, and Laura Venegas contributed greatly by adding their drumming and rattling skills to ours for the experiential CD that accompanies this book.

Gratitude also to our literary agents, Candice Fuhrman and Linda Michaels; to our editor Jill Kramer; and to Louise Hay, Reid Tracy, Jacqui Clark, Katie Williams, Jeannie Liberati, Christy Salinas, Rocky George, and everyone else at Hay House.

Thanks also to our technical support, Dan Hendrich; and to our webmaster, Nancy Brown of Studio X.

≋ ≋ ≋

Hay House Titles of Related Interest

Books

Angel Medicine, by Doreen Virtue, Ph.D.

Contacting Your Spirit Guide (book-with-CD) and *Mother God,*
both by Sylvia Browne

The God Code, by Gregg Braden, Ph.D.

Mirrors of Time, by Brian L. Weiss, M.D. (book-with CD)

Power Animals (book-with-CD) and *Sacred Ceremony,*
both by Steven D. Farmer, Ph.D.

The Reconnection, by Dr. Eric Pearl

A Stream of Dreams, by Leon Nacson

Card Decks

Archetype Cards, by Caroline Myss

Dream Cards, by Leon Nacson

Kryon Cards, by Lee Carroll

The Power of Intention Cards, by Dr. Wayne W. Dyer

≈≈

All of the above are available at your local bookstore,
or may be ordered by visiting:
Hay House USA: **www.hayhouse.com**
Hay House Australia: **www.hayhouse.com.au**
Hay House UK: **www.hayhouse.co.uk**
Hay House South Africa: **orders@psdprom.co.za**

We hope you enjoyed this Hay House book.
If you would like to receive a free catalog featuring additional Hay House
books and products, or if you would like information about the
Hay Foundation, please contact:

Hay House, Inc.
P.O. Box 5100
Carlsbad, CA 92018-5100

(760) 431-7695 or (800) 654-5126
(760) 431-6948 (fax) or (800) 650-5115 (fax)
www.hayhouse.com

≈

Published and distributed in Australia by:
Hay House Australia Pty. Ltd. • 18/36 Ralph St. • Alexandria NSW 2015
Phone: 612-9669-4299 • *Fax:* 612-9669-4144 • www.hayhouse.com.au

Published and distributed in the United Kingdom by: Hay House UK,
Ltd. • Unit 62, Canalot Studios • 222 Kensal Rd., London W10 5BN
Phone: 44-20-8962-1230 • *Fax:* 44-20-8962-1239 www.hayhouse.co.uk

Published and distributed in the Republic of South Africa by:
Hay House SA (Pty), Ltd., P.O. Box 990, Witkoppen 2068
Phone/Fax: 2711-7012233 • orders@psdprom.co.za

Distributed in Canada by: Raincoast • 9050 Shaughnessy St., Vancouver,
B.C. V6P 6E5 • *Phone:* (604) 323-7100 • *Fax:* (604) 323-2600

≈

Sign up via the Hay House USA Website to receive the Hay House
online newsletter and stay informed about what's going on with your
favorite authors. You'll receive bimonthly announcements about:
Discounts and Offers, Special Events, Product Highlights,
Free Excerpts, Giveaways, and more!
www.hayhouse.com